Post-glacial

The Selected Poetry of Robert Kroetsch

Post-glacial
The Selected Poetry of Robert Kroetsch

Selected
with an
introduction by
David Eso
and an
afterword by
Aritha van Herk

lps
LAURIER POETRY SERIES

WILFRID LAURIER
UNIVERSITY PRESS

LAURIER
Inspiring Lives.

Wilfrid Laurier University Press acknowledges the support of the Canada Council for the Arts for its publishing program. We acknowledge the financial support of the Government of Canada. This work was supported by the Research Support Fund.

Canada | Canada Council for the Arts | Conseil des arts du Canada | ONTARIO ARTS COUNCIL CONSEIL DES ARTS DE L'ONTARIO an Ontario government agency un organisme du gouvernement de l'Ontario

Library and Archives Canada Cataloguing in Publication

Title: Post-glacial : the selected poems of Robert Kroetsch / selected with an introduction by David Eso and an afterword by Aritha van Herk.
Other titles: Poems. Selections | Selected poems of Robert Kroetsch
Names: Kroetsch, Robert, 1927–2011, author. | Eso, David, 1982– editor. | Van Herk, Aritha, 1954– writer of afterword.
Series: Laurier poetry series.
Description: Series statement: Laurier poetry series | Includes bibliographical references.
Identifiers: Canadiana (print) 20190110937 | Canadiana (ebook) 20190111178 | ISBN 9781771124263 (softcover) | ISBN 9781771124287 (EPUB) | ISBN 9781771124270 (PDF)
Classification: LCC PS8521.R7 A6 2019 | DDC C811/.54—dc23

Front-cover image: *Prairie Cactus* (lithograph on paper; 30.5 x 40.6 cm) by John Snow (1911–2004).
Cover design and interior design by P.J. Woodland.

Waterloo, Ontario, Canada
www.wlupress.wlu.ca

This book is printed on FSC® certified paper. It contains postconsumer fibre, is processed chlorine free, and is manufactured using biogas energy.

FSC www.fsc.org MIX Paper from responsible sources FSC® C103567

Printed in Canada

Table of Contents

Foreword

The Laurier Poetry Series was conceived in 2002 as a means to celebrate Canadian poetry and to introduce new readers to the richness and diversity of its poets. Rather than curate another large anthology that featured only a few poems by each poet, we thought it a good idea to suggest the real range of a poet's work by enlarging the selection. Our anthology would have to comprise many volumes. But why stick with a many-volumed anthology? Why not create a series of small and affordable "selected"s? Each volume could be introduced by a knowledgeable and reader- and poet-friendly critic in greater depth than in normal anthologies, and each could provide space for the poet to respond or participate in an additional way by contributing an afterword such as no standard anthology could offer.

Readers could pick and choose which poets they wanted to explore; instructors could also pick and choose combinations of volumes in a package for their students—and could change this selection from semester to semester. And the volumes could reach an international audience. Each would also have the potential to open out onto other books by the featured poet.

That was the blueprint. The Series was launched in 2004, with Catherine Hunter's selection of the poetry of Lorna Crozier, *Before the First Word*. There have been over thirty volumes since, offering introductions to a wide range of poets and poetries, and more are in the works. The Laurier Poetry Series is now the most comprehensive collection of Canadian poetries in print anywhere. Most volumes are also available as digital editions.

The consummate professionalism of the team at Wilfrid Laurier University Press, especially Managing Editor Rob Kohlmeier, has ensured that these sometimes technically tricky volumes are presented accurately and beautifully.

What continues to inspire us about the LPS is its reception across the country. The love and art and passion and intimacy that thirty-plus editors and thirty-plus poets have brought to their volumes; the innumerable hours and conversations and meetings, the thousands of emails between and among poets and editors and the staff at WLU Press; the generous reviews in the country's journals; the reception in classrooms and beyond: all of this eloquently speaks to the joyful proliferation of poetry in Canada today.

With each new volume, LPS hopes to continue to recognize the growing provenance of this wealth, the wide range of these riches. Our poets—and their readers—deserve nothing less.

—*Brian Henderson and Neil Besner*
General Editors

Biographical Note

Robert Kroetsch (1927–2011) remains a figure of major influence in Canadian literature, due to his deep and enduring engagements in both the creative process and the literary community. His accolades include a Governor General's Award for Fiction, in 1969, in recognition of his novel *The Studhorse Man*. He was made an Officer of the Order of Canada in 2004 and received a Golden Pen Lifetime Achievement Award from the Writers Guild of Alberta in 2011. Kroetsch is well remembered as a poet, novelist, and critic with an impressive corpus of texts to his credit. He is perhaps most cited for theorizing a uniquely Canadian postmodern inheritance, imagination, and literary approach. In a disjunction typical of his often defiant and always errant intellectual style, Kroetsch developed his rich perspective on the postmodern literary ethos and its applicability to Canada while teaching in the English department of SUNY Binghamton in New York State. The author's rich legacy as a literary critic and artist is matched by the memories of those who knew him as a mentor, professor, and editor. Kroetsch's academic work brought him widespread attention from North American and international thinkers.

Such a range of achievement would not have seemed predictable to many members of his original community, although they reportedly found his bookishness conspicuous. Kroetsch was born in a homesteader's shack near the village of Heisler, southeast of Edmonton, Alberta. During his rural formative years, country-and-western songs, frontier tall tales, and an elusive Cree and Blackfoot cultural mythos were his key literary influences. Only as an adult did he find his footing as a creative writer, after his undergraduate education in English and Philosophy at the University of Alberta, after the time he spent as a labourer in the northern territories, after a master's program at Middlebury College in Vermont, and after his doctoral program in Creative Writing at the University of Iowa. Only then, in 1961, in his mid-thirties, did Kroetsch's notable output as a writer begin in earnest. By then he was installed at SUNY Binghamton and had been exposed to an exciting array of creative and critical writers. Ten years later, still at Binghamton, he would launch a seminal publication in collaboration with an iconoclast of American Empire, Dr. William Spanos. Their journal, *boundary 2*, laid the groundwork for a strictly North American interpretation of the international postmodern movement. That journal continues to issue numbers to this day (2019), long after the founders ceased their involvement.

Kroetsch's time with the journal he co-edited ended in the late 1970s, when he returned to Canada following two decades in the United States. After brief periods working in Calgary and Lethbridge, he taught in the English Department at the University of Manitoba until 1995. He spent his retirement years first on Vancouver Island and subsequently at Leduc, Alberta. The author's writings continued to appear throughout the early part of the twenty-first century, always vacillating between poetic, fictional, and critical modes, often developing a signature hybridity of form and style. In 2011, Robert Kroetsch was killed in a car accident at the age of eighty-four, while travelling home from a professional engagement in the Rocky Mountains to his home on the prairie.

Introduction

Ice Age

Robert Kroetsch was born on 26 June 1927, near the village of Heisler, Alberta. He wrote his first poem circa 1944, as a teenager. At the time of that initial experiment as a writer, he had not yet travelled far beyond his family's farm or the nearby provincial capital of Edmonton. Even so, his first poem crossed boundaries of time and space to describe a Japanese samurai warrior. A Depression-era Western Canadian farm boy with an allergy to dust, and who preferred reading books to doing manual work, young Kroetsch hit upon the samurai for the appeal of its manifold otherness. The proper subject of literature, for him at that time, had to be imported. "And here I didn't know a samurai from a hole in the ground," he reported much later, characteristically blending critical insight with folksy expression (*Poets Talk* 12). Upon the samurai's death at the end of the poem, as the author came to remember it, "The wise old moon very knowingly frowned" (12). Only years later would he venture another attempt at becoming a poet.[1]

The samurai archetype prefigured artistic tensions in the poetics that Kroetsch would develop later. The samurai's costume is a bold, individual display in which the individual hides, takes cover. The samurai (unmistakable, anonymous) disappears in plain sight. In Kroetsch's later poems, people appear in silhouette, through distorting memories, as photographed. They appear disappearing. In this, they are akin to the prairies that bred them. The poet's landscapes are of encroaching shadows, vanishing points, blinding sun, snow. Kroetsch spent his first eighteen years in those parklands, on the prairie. Land of coulees, buttes, and river valleys: the moving waters break loose from ancient seas trapped in the Rocky Mountains, bound for Hudson Bay. As a boy in that territory, he clipped black-and-white images and texts from local newspapers representing the foreign theatre of war. He pasted these cut-outs into oversized scrapbooks. Japanese or German, the imagined invader wore a uniform and helmet, not ornate armour with a scowling mask. The (lost) samurai poem is an ancient dreaming vis-à-vis the war's daily reportage, the familiar farm, the loving home. A long journey lay ahead before the writer would discover that agricultural and natural world around him as the stuff of literature.

Kroetsch became a poet again in a scrapbook created after the war's end. On facing pages, he pasted his "first article" and his "first poem." The latter was published in *The Gateway*, a University of Alberta student newspaper. "Revelations" listens in on two male students surreptitiously reading from the diary of a female co-ed, a dire mistake committed on purpose:

> "Dear diary," wrote the wily maid,
> "Poor Tommy's monthly cheque is done,
> And Bill can't have the car this week,
> So that leaves only one.
>
> "I know he is a dreary dope:
> His talk is dull, his humour grim.
> I know he has a car and cash—
> I'm going back to him..."
>
> Now, when he read these fiendish words,
> One scholar moaned, "Good-bye, my friend."
> And wrapped a towel around his neck—
> His name was at the end. (Papers, 775/04.25 22.2)

A work of juvenilia, "Revelations" nonetheless contains prophetic elements. It shows how early on Kroetsch felt his impulse toward refracted, depreciating self-portraiture. He would later describe his work as adding up to an anti-autobiography: "one in which I just cannot accept any of the conventions of autobiography" (Neuman and Wilson 208).[2] Sprung from the family farm and landed at university, he created the doggerel poetry of "Revelations" from his immediate, suddenly bustling social environment. From this point on, he would continue to depict encounters with friends, relatives, lovers, and strangers, just as he would continue to write in an upending, comic mode. As a poet, he preferred short words (for their oral tones) as opposed to learned vocabulary. Despite these predictors of his later style, "Revelations" parrots the coy melodrama and singsong rhyme scheme of an earlier generation's versifiers, successful Canadian poets like Robert Service. In that respect, Kroetsch had much uncovering and rewriting left ahead.

As an undergraduate in the late 1940s, he enrolled in a class on creative writing, not yet a mainstream subject of study on North American university campuses. The writerly memoir *A Likely Story* (1995) relates his experience of the course's first meeting. He felt intimidated by a room of soldiers newly returned from active duty in Europe. Fifty years later, he recalled the students' round of introductions:

> One student was a former fighter pilot who mentioned in passing that he could not turn out his light at night. . . . When my turn came I said I was fresh out of high school and just finished helping with the harvest. We were heavily under the influence of Hemingway at the time, and believed that to be a writer one had to go out and seek dangerous experiences. I had been nowhere, I felt. I had done nothing, I felt. (*Likely Story* 144)

He froze, withdrew. Whatever could a farm boy from Heisler find to write about?

> Birds in
> poplar bluffs on open
> prairie. Orioles and wild
> canaries. Bird-busy
> sloughs, surrounded by
> willows. Mallards and
> snipes and red-winged
> blackbirds.[3]

Where was the poetry in all that? "After class I went and dropped the course," Kroetsch wrote, "and registered in a course called Victorian Poetry" (144). Upon graduation, he went north for six years. He went for adventure and to labour: on the Mackenzie River in the Northwest Territories and at Goose Bay, Labrador. He went to reinvent himself as the kind of man modern literature might celebrate. He produced no poems during that period, and a cyclical pattern of surge and withdrawal would mark his engagement with poetry for the rest of his life.

Interglacial

The poetic impulse revisited Kroetsch again during his thirties: a time of life when whimsy and idealism are supposed to make way for more practical matters. As a graduate student of creative writing, following his time in the north, he had written primarily fiction. Then, during the 1960s, he closely followed the artistic developments in Canadian literature from afar, while working as a Professor of English at the State University of New York's Binghamton campus. In that decade, Canadian poetry gained unprecedented attention through the work of poets like Margaret Atwood, Leonard Cohen, Irving Layton, and Michael Ondaatje, among others. Concurrently, Kroetsch began to publish his own poetic experiments in Canadian magazines and literary journals. Ignoring the earlier "Revelations," the journal *Prism* called his "Letter to a Friend's Wife," which appeared in a 1961 issue, "the first [poem] he has published" (Papers, MsC 27 24.14). Others appeared regularly over the course of that decade. Kroetsch's archive offers an omnibus assemblage of his ephemeral verses, many of which never appeared in later volumes of his poetry. "Tourist from Toronto," from James Reany's journal *alphabet* (1967), is one example chosen for the present selection. Kroetsch's scattered poems of the 1960s are short narratives, romantic lyrics, prairie pastorals, elegies, confessions, and satires. But for all this activity, Kroetsch did not publish a volume of poetry until 1975. Yet he published three novels during the 1960s.

By the early 1970s, Kroetsch was teaching graduate courses in contemporary literature and had introduced the study of creative writing to the SUNY Binghamton campus. He also co-founded with William Spanos the journal *boundary 2*, which was the first periodical in North America committed to exploring the newly conceived "postmodern" theory of literature. Literary postmodernism was to be a playful and even irreverent raging, set against the relentless seriousness of high modernism. *boundary 2* opened its first issue (1972) with an introduction to the cultural criticism of Michel Foucault, penned by Edward Said. This decision shows how deeply the editors were immersed in contemporary intellectual currents, even though they drew much inspiration for their project from an earlier source, German philosopher Martin Heidegger. While Spanos focused mainly on selecting the journal's essays, it fell to Kroetsch to gather the poems. He also acted as general editor for a special issue on Canadian literature published in the fall of 1974. Working as an editor and professor in the United States, he continued to give readings and publish his poems in Canadian venues. His extended residence in the US (and academia) lent imaginative space for him to reconstruct the rural world of his Alberta childhood.

During the steep rise of *boundary 2*, the poet developed ever-richer means to represent a poetics of prairie landscape and to convey the common discourse of his community around Heisler, typified by tall tales and country-and-western songs. Then, following a 1974 visit to Nanaimo, British Columbia, the ice dam broke. Two different influences produced this breakthrough. First, his intellectual activity related to *boundary 2* had exposed him to an emergent postmodern imagination that undermined the stability of a hierarchical literary culture. The second influence was that an accumulation of trips to various Canadian locales as a visiting writer helped him explore a persona as a rollicking pan–Western Canadian. Experience with the people and places of British Columbia and the prairie provinces broadened his sense of home and belonging—even though he defined the Western Canadian experience as "a loner's trip" (Papers, 775/04.25 17).[4] To John Marshall, editor of the journal *Island*, he wrote of the poetic epiphany he experienced after returning to the United States from Vancouver Island:

> Hey, goddamn, after swearing off poetry forever while walking through the rain forests of Vancouver Island I came back here [to Binghamton] and last week end started my inevitable long poem. Will try to send you a section for response. I've cracked it, the absolute problem of wherewhyness, the uninventing into form. The soulself seeking/speaking. (Papers, 334/84.1, 3.59)

This letter describes a watershed moment. A broadening identification with Western Canadian geography and dialect had combined productively with a deepening understanding of deconstructive poetics vis-à-vis the international postmodernism explored by Foucault, Said, and Spanos. Through these paired phenomenological and theoretical influences, Kroetsch uncovered the endlessly expansive form in which he would excel—the long poem. By working in that form, he entered the territory of those American poets he taught at Binghamton, for example Charles Olson via the *Maximus Poems* and John Berryman via *The Dream Songs*. Another influential poet for Kroetsch was Wallace Stevens, who wrote expansive, sequential poetry such as the thirty-three sections of "The Man with the Blue Guitar." But Kroetsch also borrowed from William Carlos Williams the dictum to write from "a local pride," via the long poem *Paterson* (2). This paradoxically foreign influence validated and renewed ongoing investigations into his early experience of a particular homeplace. He soon found that other Canadian writers of long poems had arrived ahead of him with their own experimental depictions of place: Dennis Lee, Daphne Marlatt, bp Nichol.

For the next decade, Kroetsch collections from Canadian small presses appeared regularly, each gathered around long poems and serial poems. After *The Ledger* and *Stone Hammer Poems* (both 1975) came *Seed Catalogue* (1977) and *The Sad Phoenician* (1979). He kept up this pace until *Advice to My Friends* and *Excerpts from the Real World* in the mid-1980s and then swore off poetry (again). Across the range of his long poems and serial poems, Kroetsch tried out various ways to combine daily experience and common language with intellectual reflection and complex undertones. He writes as a storyteller, memoirist, correspondent, documentarian, critic, and trickster. The long poem gave him a way of relating his perceptions without making final statements. The form allows for recurrence, contradiction, elaboration, and revisions. "Sketches of a Lemon," included in this collection, performs a necessary resetting of perception when we look, double-take, triple-take, and so on. In other words, when we respect and reconceive those not-so-simple places and objects that surround us.

Post-glacial

One can usefully think of Kroetsch's slow development as well as his imaginatively preserved childhood—frozen in time—as figurative Ice Ages, relative to his surge of writing long poems in the 1970s and 80s. That hot streak is represented by "Stone Hammer Poem" and "Delphi: Commentary" in the present selection. During the 1990s and early 2000s, the fledgling North American postmodernism he had helped to incubate gained a dominant place in literary culture. Whereas postmodern theory developed toward abstract philosophical, political, and international concerns, Kroetsch's writing became increasingly embedded in his experience, his own community, and his representations of local or regional settings. Accordingly, he came to use the term postmodern less and less, even as his poetry became more and more experimental. In the 1990s and 2000s, he moved from long poems published by small presses to ever more disjunctive poetry chapbooks from obscure publishers. Chapbooks represented in the present selection include *Revisions of a Letter Already Sent* from DisOrientation (now defunct), *Writer's Block* from Greenboathouse Press, and the *David Thompson* and *Mrs. David Thompson* chapbooks from Wrinkle Press. Following the start of the new millennium, Kroetsch published his most experimental book of poetry: *The Hornbooks of Rita K.* (2001). Ostensibly written by a manifested subpersonality of the author—and by her editor, archivist, and spurned lover Raymond—it vies for the Oddest Book Ever Shortlisted for the Governor General's Literary Award. Having run out of ways to subvert himself, Kroetsch returned to experimentation with short lyric poems for his final collection, *Too Bad: Sketches Toward a Self-Portrait* (2010), published in the year before his death.

Kroetsch's errant career in poetry is characterized by slow-moving divergences and a focus on place (shaped and shaping). For these reasons, I suggest "post-glacial" as an alternative to the classification "postmodern." A term borrowed from geography, post-glacial refers to the Holocene (the past ten thousand years and counting), the present moment (despite the continued presence of high-altitude glaciers), and equally to an indeterminate future period (a possible future wherein no glaciers remain). Post-glacial refigures in spatiotemporal terms postmodern concepts such as trace, spectre, or the presence of absence—concepts promoted by Jacques Derrida and others. "Trace," in its postmodern sense, means that the past is never past. Drumlins, erratics, eskers, and even the flatness of the great plains are the visible work of Pleistocene ice sheets. That past haunts the present through the presence of year-round ice high up in the Rocky Mountains. These are post-glacial times we live in, although some glaciers remain. Past is now. Future arrives ahead of time. Glaciers do not melt. Ice melts. Glaciers retreat, recreating the land that remains always subject to revision. Similarly, the voices of the poet's parents recur with increasing clarity, posthumously. Another parallel: the great literary traditions of history survive in Kroetsch's work—quest, romance, satire—through subversive response to the weight of those inherited forms.

The present selection does not offer an "essential" or "best of" poetry collection. Instead, it draws on a blend of accessible and confounding poems from across Kroetsch's writing career. The ordering of poems in *Post-glacial* does not follow the usual structure of advancing according to date of composition. Rather, this unique sequencing of poems uncovers the poet's voice by beginning with moods of morning and spring, moving through undulating gradations to shades of night and mourning. A particularly tricky volume to draw from was *The Hornbooks of Rita K.*

Rita Kleinhart represents one of the writers Robert K. might have become had he been born female and had (s)he remained a permanent citizen of central Alberta, rather than having departed at a young age to become an urbanite and academic. Given their author's persistent fluctuations in form and style, each poem in *Post-glacial* represents a different version of the writer becoming.

—David Eso

Notes

1 Kroetsch spoke about this poem before a group of high-school students at Alberta's Canmore Collegiate, in 2011. See the YouTube video "High School Q&A in Canmore with Robert Kroetsch & Others."

2 Douglas Reimer uses the term "anti-autobiography" to describe Kroetsch's poem "Seed Catalogue" (53).

3 See "Lonesome Writer Diptych," page 17 of this volume.

4 This phrase comes from a journal entry for 26 January 1971. In it, Kroetsch compares the "free-wheelers of the west" to "eastern nationalists" who enjoy "the protection, the restraint of society" (Papers, 775/04.25 17).

References

Berryman, John. *The Dream Songs*. New York: Farrar, Straus and Giroux, 1969.

Butling, Pauline. *Poets Talk*. Edmonton: University of Alberta Press, 2005.

"High School Q&A in Canmore with Robert Kroetsch & Others." *YouTube*, uploaded by *filling Station* magazine, 23 June 2011, https://www.youtube.com/watch?v=lf2N6qHG6Kw.

Kroetsch, Robert. *A Likely Story*. Red Deer, AB: Red Deer College Press, 1995.

Olson, Charles. *The Maximus Poems*. New York: Jargon/Corinth, 1960.

Neuman, Shirley, and Robert Wilson, eds. *Labyrinths of Voice: Conversations with Robert Kroetsch*. Edmonton: NeWest Press, 1982.

The Robert Kroetsch Papers. Accessions 775/04.25, 334/84.1, and MsC 27. University of Calgary Special Collections, Calgary, Alberta.

Reimer, Douglas. "Heideggerian Elements in *Seed Catalogue*." *Open Letter* 5–6 (1996): 51–63.

Said, Edward. "Michel Foucault and the Intellectual Imagination." *boundary 2* 1.1 (1972): 1–36.

Stevens, Wallace. *The Man with the Blue Guitar and Other Poems*. New York: Knopf, 1937.

Williams, William Carlos. *Paterson*. New York: New Directions, 1963.

Pirate Story

My father was wrecking an old prairie house
to salvage the lumber. He looked like a pirate,
up there on the roof ridge, swinging a hammer.

I made a sword from a plastering lath.
The gold I stole from the Spanish
was the gold they stole from the Incas.

We were in cahoots, my father and I,
he attacking the weathered house,
I attacking the ship he rode.

My sword was two-edged. My father
looked like a pirate. What does the son
of a pirate do, after the ship is demolished?

Having a Word with Columbus: A Song for Ed Dyck

You were right, Columbus,
to try and trick us,
                                        The Americas are not

    here, the gold of the Inca gods
    has not been stolen,
    the fish of the Grand Banks
    still swim, inviolate and thick,
    in the cold green water,
    the forests of Lake Erie
    ring loud with calling birds,
    the buffalo of the Great Plains
    graze in their millions,
    the wide whales, splendiferous and fat,
    sing their way
    through the Inland Passage,
    the salmon leap totemic
    over coastal villages.

Thief and liar, Columbus,
you taught us everything
we know. What a pity Amerigo

Vespucci pulled that fast one,
got the illusion named
after himself.

There is a World

good morning, monday   you don't
look so hot yourself   you one-eyed
bastard   here in the hard west

we hold each other's bodies/   here
in the coyote night   we howl
the dawn   is just another

dawn/   don't look so self-important
I know she left: I heard the car
too, the quick gravel: it was

a short summer   those three nights
god, I was drunk somewhere   somewhere
we argued   against mortality, made love;

nobody warned us   there is a world
I hear it   the blackbird dawn
flocking the day loud and   hullabaloo

the slow stenographers   caw
the epitaph: I miss you/
what can I add: my bed, hollow

the ring   the coop of heaven
hangs on a hollow sky   a hawk:
I/wishing you here   hold me

free/   my cock's crow to the
rising predator   the scalding day:
there is a world/   I miss you

Tourist from Toronto

1

The Mennonites in Alberta make chokecherry wine.
They wear black hats. They do not believe
in electricity.

The Lutherans in Alberta wear green fedoras.
They believe in electricity.
They do not make chokecherry wine.

The atheists in Alberta make electricity.
They do not cover their heads. They drink
chokecherry wine, beer, scotch, gin, rye, rum.

2 At the White Rose
station   I
ask for the key
to the men's john
I lock my
self in   I
invest a half
dollar & get 3
safes
        and I
(fillerup please)
just before paying
insert
1 cent in the
            vertical
            black
            slot:

3 You, sir, weigh
177
8
9 lbs: Come
what may
you are a fine
addition, sir,
to any rope that
hangs, a born
tosspot,
rounder
and b.s. artist
: but never sleep,
sir, till the cock
crows: you are
going
on a long trip.

4

The Presbyterians in Alberta prefer
the Pontiac to the MG. They dream of wading
(weeping, other) in the Firth of Clyde.

Socrates would not leave Athens.
He believed in anamnesis.
He wore no hat, apparently; he drank.

Are we there yet?

I stopped in this place in shortgrass country.

I asked the waitress, How far is it to the world?

She said, Two days of hard driving. Unless you're traveling by horse.

I was puzzled. In that case? I said.

In that case, she said, you've just arrived. What can I get you?

She allowed me a smile that wasn't on the menu. I decided to gamble.

Bring me, I said, a bucket of water. And a small pail of oats.

as the flowers see them

clink cLink *clI*nNK KLiNKK
at the door :   miners
dirty faces where lamps
in hand they land & peer

picks in hand apparently
they are pears (prickly)
halos about their heads
what you see of them
lamps shrug rooms open
work till their bowels burn
dry faces bowls of gold
          bug eyed with joy
they come back singing
          eyes they tip
            toe through the tulips
set pearls that pop or fizz
they are the lilies of the fields
they sing   loud as a welsh choir

Stone Hammer Poem

1.

This stone
become a hammer
of stone, this maul

is the colour
of bone (no,
bone is the colour
of this stone maul).

The rawhide loops
are gone, the
hand is gone, the
buffalo's skull
is gone;

the stone is
shaped like the skull
of a child.

2.

This paperweight on my desk

where I begin
this poem   was

found in a wheatfield
lost (this hammer,
this poem).

Cut to a function,
this stone was
(the hand is   gone—

3.

Grey, two-headed,
the pemmican maul

fell from the travois or
a boy playing   lost it in
the prairie wool or
a woman   left it in
the brain of a buffalo or

it is a million
years older than
the hand that
chipped stone or
raised slough
water (or blood) or

4.

This stone maul
was found.

In the field
my grandfather
thought
was his

my father
thought was his

5.

It is a stone
old as the last
Ice Age, the
retreating/the
recreating ice,
the retreating
buffalo, the
retreating Indians

(the saskatoons bloom
white (infrequently
the chokecherries the
highbush cranberries the

pincherries bloom
white along the barbed
wire fence (the
pemmican   winter

6.

This stone maul
stopped a plough
long enough for one
Gott im Himmel.

The Blackfoot (the
Cree?) not

finding the maul
cursed.

? did he curse
? did he try to
go back
? what happened
I have to/I want
to know (not know)
? WHAT HAPPENED

7.

The poem
is the stone
chipped and hammered
until it is shaped
like the stone
hammer, the maul.

8.

Now the field is
mine because
I gave it
(for a price)

to a young man
(with a growing son)
who did not

notice that the land
did not belong

to the Indian who
gave it to the Queen
(for a price) who
gave it to the CPR
(for a price) which
gave it to my grandfather
(for a price) who
gave it to my father
(50 bucks an acre
Gott im Himmel I cut
down all the trees I
picked up all the stones) who

gave it to his son
(who sold it)

9.

This won't
surprise you.

My grandfather
lost the stone maul.

10.

My father (retired)
grew raspberries.
He dug in his potato patch.
He drank one glass of wine
each morning.
He was lonesome
for death.

He was lonesome for the
hot wind on his face, the smell
of horses, the distant
hum of a threshing machine,
the oilcan he carried, the weight
of a crescent wrench in his hind pocket.

He was lonesome for his absent
son and his daughters,
for his wife, for his own
brothers and sisters and
his own mother and father.

He found the stone maul
on a rockpile in the
north-west corner of what
he thought of
as his wheatfield.

He kept it (the
stone maul) on the railing
of the back porch in
a raspberry basket.

11.

I keep it
on my desk
(the stone).

Sometimes I use it
in the (hot) wind
(to hold down paper)

smelling a little of cut
grass or maybe even of
ripening wheat or of
buffalo blood hot
in the dying sun.

Sometimes I write
my poems for that

stone hammer.

Taste

When my mother was impatient with me
she called me RPK. RPK, she said, Leave
those cookies alone. They're for the threshers.

I stole three macaroons and a jam-jam
and ran from the house. I had a place where
I liked to hide. It was in the shelter belt.

I knew my mother knew the place. That's why
I went there. I wanted her to come find me.
I waited. I could hear the threshers unhitching

their teams of horses, coming in for supper.
I waited and I waited. I ate the cookies.
I couldn't name the taste. I'm still waiting.

Projected Visit

The crops are off
now, the harvest
done: in Alberta
even the sun is
bleached
by the shortening
day; the blackbirds,

lost in a prairie
graveyard, grieve
on a barbed wire
fence; the wind
walks in the night,
trying for unlocked
doors…

        But what if
the first snow falls:
if the partridge does not
chirr from the stubbled
field; if the fence
has not held; if my
great tall
        father
his eyes
        forgiving
an errant son
does not stoop
from the grave to
love me   home?

Spring Harvest

1.

That fall   we were snowed in
while the grain stood in stooks

and all winter long the mice
multiplied in the stooks   the owls

came to the drifted fields
as if the white North was emptied

of owls   as if Kenojuak herself
had created   their pitiless eyes.

2.

One teamster was too proud   that spring
to tie his pant legs shut; I saw him
swatting at his balls as if
his prick itself had turned   into a mouse.

My aunt   cooking for threshers
(and scared to death of mice)
noticed a wisp of smoke,
told me to climb the windmill.

And looking out squint-eyed from my perch
over that circle of prairie and slough hole,
I saw the flames (like a plague of red
mice) coming north under a south wind.

3.

We were half blind
in the smoke, swatting
with wet sacks,
the flames leaping
each fire line   before
it was ploughed

wide enough
or black;
            the earth
and sky   hinged
on a red
tongue
as if   we had ourselves
been snatched up,
would be devoured.

4.

The flames harvested that crop.
The owls must have gone
back North on the south wind.
The men, forgetting their dreams,
got on with the spring sowing.

But I remember those owls
at night   on the silent snow
and the fat mice   squealing
out of the flames   as if
each stook   was a burning bush.

Lonesome Writer Diptych

1

When my father was in his
prime and I was a boy of
eight, I decided one morn-
ing to take his pocket
watch apart—and to put it
back together again—
without his noticing.

He had left his watch on
the dresser in my parents'
bedroom.

1

2

Time to me was a sound.
I could hold it to my ear
and count its passing. Yes,
time passed. I had learned
that. Time past was some-
thing else. The hands of a
clock were called hands.
The face of a clock was
called a face.

2

As a child I memorized
the exquisite temptation
of silence.

It was a confusing park-
lands silence. Birds in
popular bluffs on open
prairie. Orioles and wild
canaries. Bird-busy
sloughs, surrounded by
willows. Mallards and
snipes and red-winged
blackbirds. A wide, quiet
place, full of the sounds
of the sky.

3

Why did my mother let
me take the watch from
the dresser and out onto
the verandah on the east
side of the house? The
sun, of course, was hot,
that summer morning, on
the verandah. There was a

3

table on the verandah that my mother used in spring to place her house plants on. Or her seedlings. I sat at that table to work on the watch that I was going to dismantle and reassemble.

4

We lived on a farm 100 miles south and east of Edmonton, near the Battle River. Rivers are maps of Alberta, maps that shift, change, alter the landscape itself.

It was the Battle River, with its deep, post-glacial valley, carving the landscape into form, that defined our parklands location. My father was gone all the way to Edmonton. It was a full day's journey, going to Edmonton and returning. I had a whole day in which to work on the watch. But why did I want to take apart and reassemble my father's watch without his knowing?

4

One Sunday morning in a pasture by the Battle River some of us kids were playing rodeo and I got onto a young bull that bucked—and then I got off. I got off abruptly and violently. Getting off hurt. It hurt a lot. There are two varieties of cactus that grow in the coulee hills of the Battle River. Pincushion and prickly pear. And hardpan is hard. I thought I might be dying and said so. Someone told me to get up off my ass and get back onto the bull. In a rebellious moment I said I was not going to get back onto the bull, I was going to be a writer.

5

My hometown makes an appearance in the text of Aritha van Herk's novel

5

I think I expected to find
in that watch the future
itself.

6

My mother brought me
milk, oatmeal cookies.
She lured me into the
house for lunch, then, in
her quiet way of pretend-
ing not to see, let me go
back to my task. And tak-
ing the watch apart had
been easy. As the after-
noon wore on, I saw I was
going to have a bit of
trouble putting it back
together again.

7

I sometimes see myself, as
a writer now, still sitting
at that table on the veran-
dah, still trying to get the

No Fixed Address. The nar-
rator makes mention of a
ball diamond and a cafe,
this in a chapter called
"Memento Mori." Aritha
van Herk and I grew up
on opposite sides of the
Battle River. I had depart-
ed before she arrived.

And yet we heard each
other's voices in the deep
coulees, on the alkali flats,
on the shores of Dried
Meat Lake. Voices become
their own bodies. Or is it
the other way round? I
forget.

6

Fictional characters allow
us to test ourselves—I am
tempted to say, text our-
selves. Arachne, the hero-
ine of *No Fixed Address*, is a
woman of no fixed
address who is compul-
sively at home.

watch back together
before I hear the sound of
a car that I cannot yet see,
before the far tower of
dust lifts itself above the
horizon.

8

Had my father left his watch behind on purpose? Did I catch a glimpse of a smile on my mother's face when I asked her if I could take it from their bedroom, out onto the verandah that faced onto the road, just—as I so carefully put it—just to play?

9

For all our contemporary skepticism, we cannot resist reading the world as a small allegory of this or that. A river has something to do with time, but what does it have to do with a watch?

10

It was late in the afternoon of that hot summer day when my father drove

7

I spent much of my life writing novels that I thought would enable me to give Alberta the slip.

Create a replica and enter in.

Skin out.

8

Fred Wah writes from the context I think of as noise. He was trained as a jazz musician and in that manifestation learned to shape noise into the music at the heart of thinking. He surprises us with the elegant shapes that inhabit multitudinous and discordant sounds.

9

To our surprise, in the parklands, we discover that even geography is not a certainty on this fickle planet. Riding the buck-

into the yard, back from the city, his mysterious purpose—I forget what it was—accomplished. My mother had been listening, too, for the car, watching. She went out into the yard to meet my father.

Ordinarily I would have beat her to the car. She went out to the car and spoke to my father before he opened the door.

ing bull of plate tectonics, we hang on for dear life to a floating world.

10

It is not possible to write an autobiography. By the time I learned that lesson it was too late for me to avoid the necessity.

The poet Doug Barbour, trying to escape into the language of absent occasion, turns space into a road. Monty Reid, that geographer of the mind's discontent, maps the blunt imaginary.

Robert Hilles, in the graphing of a moment's enduring pain, finds the long poem, even the lyric narrative of dislocated time.

By borrowing fragments of other lives I borrow an autobiography of my own. I disappear, only to discover that I have once again made a turn in the labyrinth and met the monster with the body of a human and the head of a bull.

11

My father came up the steps of the verandah and looked at the table and at his watch. I wasn't looking at him, so I can only guess now that he looked at his watch.

"To bad," he said. "Too bad about the watch. I was going to give it to you."

12

He had made it home, just in the nick of time, for supper.

Or is it the other way round? I forget.

11

There was for me, at one time, literally no way in which I could imagine Alberta as the stuff of a novel. I went to Montreal. In Montreal I rented a garret, because I knew writers were supposed to live in garrets. I had read as much somewhere in a book.

12

The promise of mountains. The promise of glaciers. But those promises are without pastoral implications. They announce a fugitive concern. By hiding one insists that one is part of the landscape.

Sydney

Realizing that light, not dark, is the poet's affliction, he gives himself the Governor General's Award For Not Writing Poetry for the year 1999.

He leaves his hotel in Kings Cross and goes to see the art show, ORIGINS ORIGINALITY + BEYOND, the Biennale of Sydney 1986.

He stops first at the Art Gallery of New South Wales, then buys a map and finds his way to Pier 2/3, on Walsh Bay, where the larger works are on display in an old pier building.

Magdalena Abakanowicz, SEVEN STANDING FIGURES
Robert Adrian, 76 AIRPLANES
Julie Brown-Rrap, BREAK AND ENTER—EXHIBITS 1–4

Braco Dimitrijevíc, MEMORIES OF COLUMBUS, FRIEND
Richard Killeen, TIME TO CHANGE THE GREEK HERO
Wolfgang Laib, THE SIXTY-THREE RICE MEALS FOR A STONE

Vivienne Shark Lewitt, LAST NIGHT I DREAMED I WENT TO
MANDALAY AGAIN
Rainer Mang, DEUTSCHER MANN SUCHT WAS
Carlo Maria Mariani, GUARDASI IN UNO SPECCHIO CELESTE
(LOOKING AT ONESELF IN A HEAVENLY MIRROR)

Marta Minujin, THE BOOK'S PARTHENON
Luigi Ontani, YOUNG MAN WITH FRUITS
Therese Oulton, MORTAL COIL

Yumiko Sugano, WHALE'S GENERATION
Masami Teraoka, HANAUMA BAY SERIES/CAMERA CREW
AND BLOWHOLE I

Michael Nelson Tjakamarra, POSSUM DREAMING

Anon, Canada, 1927, SELF-PORTRAIT OF POET OF
THROWING IN THE TOWEL, EH?

Wellington, New Zealand

Realizing he is done with poetry, he goes to a museum to see a reconstruction of an extinct New Zealand bird, a bird that was flightless, huge, possibly the largest bird (height to 12 feet) that ever lived, the Giant Moa. Now how's that for self-pity?

The poem as quotation:

> Merino Sheep: The oldest and most numerous breed in the world. Originated in Spain or North Africa. First sheep in N.Z. Captain Cook brought four in 1773, they did not survive. Wool: fine fibre, used in quality woollen and worsted fabrics.
>
> Feel free to stroke Lindale's stock through the fence.
>
> Murray Gray Cattle: This breed came about by accident when in 1902 a Shorthorn cow was crossed with a black Angus bull, the result a grey calf, a Mulberry. This unwanted cow survived to produce 12 Mulberries. The name change came in the 1960s. Very adaptable, the breed has prospered in N.Z. conditions
>
> Sheep and cattle may nibble for nuts but will not bite.

The poem as evasion.
The poem as resignation.
The poem as a net
that drowns fish.
The poem as a postcard
sent directly to the sun.
The poem as POET TREE.

Delphi Commentary

: the calendar of *anthropos*
is the clown-god's whip*

It seems that from the beginning the sanctuary of Delphi has been the object of innumerable plots.

– Pausanias, 2nd Century A.D.

What can we say for certain? The day was sure to be a clear one; Meg reported that at breakfast. She had, while her sister was in the shower, taken a picture of the Parthenon. The Hotel Herodion is under the Acropolis. My room faced on the walled garden where late-night drinkers whispered in various tongues to the grape vines and the waiters. Meg took a picture. The window framed the picture she would take: high on the sunlit rock, the Parthenon in profile to the August-morning light. I was drinking too much coffee while my daughters, Laura and Meg, ate honeydew melon and sampled the feta. We had not finished our eating when the driver came into the breakfast room, his eyes naming us.

*fragment from "The Eggplant Poems"

: the glyph on the broken stone
raises the eye, reads the tongue

We were, it turned out, taking a bus to catch our bus.
We were the only passengers, my two American daughters
and I, until the driver stopped at
another hotel and a Japanese lady
came up the stairwell of the bus,
an elegant lady so small our greetings
went over her head. She was wearing a
soft white hat with two plastic buttons
pinned discreetly on the left side, one
of them reading, OUZO POWER. She had
brought along her smile. She put it
on. The streets of Athens were morning
streets; I wanted coffee at a sidewalk
cafe. But the driver thumbed his horn
at all of Constitution Square. We
turned into a side street. We were
unloaded from the bus, for sorting
according to language:

Greek
English
German
French
Italian

Pausanias's Description of Greece,
translated with a commentary by J. G.
Frazer (Macmillan and Co., Limited,
St. Martin's Street, London, 1913):
All the twenty-seven names of the Olympic
trophy occur on the Delphic trophy, but
the order is somewhat different, and on
the Delphic trophy there are four names
... which, if Pausanias's list is
correct, did not appear on the Olympic
trophy. How are these discrepancies
to be explained?

Lacedaemonians
Athenians
Corinthians
Tegeans
Sicyonians
Aeginetans
Megarians
Epidaurians
Orchomenians
Phliasians
Troezenians
Hermionians
Tirynthians
Plataeans
Thespians
Mycenaeans
Ceans
Melians
Tenians
Naxians
Eretrians
Chalcidians
Canadians
Styrians
Eleans
Potidaeans
Leucadians
Anactorians
Cythnians
Siphnians
Ambraciots
Lepreans

:   the chariot fell
      into the sky

and, going to Delphi, going to Delphi, I had expected
to ask a question, the three of us on the bus, the morning
ride, into morning, my daughters with me, there on the road
to Delphi

going to Delphi, a father, his two daughters

Laura, entering college in
the fall: We could ask if
acid rain will dissolve the
world, make it as pure as
glass, as empty.

going to Delphi,
a question, seeking
a speaker

into a forest
of olive trees

going to Delphi

and Margaret, to her father:
Why do you want to be a tree?

I want to be an *olive* tree, I explained, not just any old
tree; one of those ancient olive trees, with holes clean
through the trunk, where you can see out the other side.
To what? Meg said. To other olive trees, I explained

going to Delphi

:   the [Pythian] silence

and the voice on the loudspeaker system:

Marathon. That place over there [that we've just passed, that you almost saw] is Marathon. The messenger, when the Persians were defeated, ran all the way to Athens. They had no Key Tour buses then [laughter]. He ran those twenty-two miles [the precious words, locked on his tongue]. His message spoken [the victory spoken, the city saved] he fell down dead.

and the voice on the loudspeaker system:

Thebes. That small town that you see just over there was once [famous, I did not dare add, for its fresh water, for its abundance of trees] a city. It was levelled stone by stone by the Macedonians [of Alexander the Great].

and if

and when I fell asleep,
lulled by the bus, and my
head tilted and teetered,
almost fell off, Meg woke
me up with her

[daughterly]

giggling

and if
the [abandoned]
poem
speaks

:   silence   is a form of periphrasis

We stopped for coffee. The bus stopped. We filed out,
all of us, out of the bus, through categories of trade,
T-shirts, postcards, cups and saucers with pictures on
them of Mt. Parnassus.

I sat down, over coffee, under the big windows, by a woman
from Australia. She was in her late seventies, travelling
alone, alone for six weeks, in Europe. She praised the
beauty of my daughters. Her eyebrows were soft white
caterpillars that moved on her forehead when she spoke.
We talked of weather, of crops, the woman from Australia
and I. Her husband, long dead, had been a wheat farmer.
During the war, she explained, he had trained in Canada.
Aircrew. He had seen the wheatfields of Canada. He was
killed in a crash. That was her first husband. Her second
husband, he too was dead.

Pausanias, the ordinary
traveller, of whom Sir
James Frazer said: *Without
him the ruins of Greece
would for the most part be
a labyrinth without a clue,
a riddle without an
answer.*

What did he eat, along the
way? What drinks did he
stop for? Did he meet old
ladies who spoke to strangers
of husbands dead in the wars?
What was the road like,
without buses? Were the
washrooms clean? Did fathers
travel with their daughters,
and weep in the night for
love?

Pausanias, the ordinary
traveller:

(Bk. VII ACHAIA, Ch. XXIII, Pt. I) *I have also heard say
that the water of the Selemnus is a cure for love in man
and woman, for they wash in the river and forget their
love. If there is any truth in this story, great riches
are less precious to mankind than the water of the Selemnus.*

: the holes in the cheese contain the cheese

And behind us, on the seats behind us, talking across the aisle as we talked across the aisle, three women from New Jersey: three braggart women, baggy-faced, rich-bitch clothing and one of the three painted to look like a child,

all of them jangling their gold in our ears, and asking each other: How will we get our stuff through Customs? They schemed and plotted, one deciding which three blouses to wear through Customs, another planning to fill her brassiere (How will we get our stuff through Customs? with Turkish coins. They heard from a conversation behind us that the site of Delphi is all up and down, not level. We should have stayed in Athens and gone shopping, they told each other. And my young daughters looked daggers across the aisle to me, intending their glances to swerve, become eagles, become thunder-bolts …

Sir James Frazer: … *the Delphians decreed that for the future the oracles should be pronounced, not by a virgin, but by a woman over fifty years of age, attired as a virgin.*

Sir James Frazer, in response to Pausanias's doubt (he believed in the gods, in the heroes) as to whether the Celts possessed an art of divination (x, xxi, 2):

The Celts practised divination by means of human sacrifices; the victim was stabbed in the back and omens were drawn from his convulsions … Justin mentions that, before engaging in battle with Antigonous, king of Macedonia, the Gauls slew victims and drew omens from their entrails.

: eat your breakfast before lunch;
buy shoes for both feet

on the dangerous road to Delphi, Oedipus, King of Thebes:

The Cleft Way

From this point the high
road to Delphi grows
steeper and more difficult
to a man on foot. Many and
diverse are the tales told
about Delphi, and still
more about the oracle of
Apollo. (Pausanias. His
scattered Greece under
Roman rule.)

It is always that way, the poem, the abandoned poem, in
which the hero, seeking the answer to the impossible
question, seeking the impossible question, takes to the road.
Hero. Eros. The evasion that is the meeting. The impossible
road.

It is always that way.
Swing with the road's high
curve, upward, past the
bauxite mines (spilling the
mountain ochre and orange).
And the first glimpse, over
the fell and crisscross
hills, a gap, agape; and a
shaped stone (broken); and
on its slant of (shaping)
stone, under the sky-high
cliff:

The city of Delphi stands wholly on a slope, and not only the city, but also the sacred close of Apollo. The close is very spacious, and is situated at the highest part of the city … I will mention what seemed to me the most noteworthy of the votive offerings.

We blundered our way out of the bus,
into a line where we might buy tickets,
at seventy drachmas each, a ticket
blank on one side, on the other an
almost pale green, to the left in grey
and white a drawing of the head of
Socrates, balding, bearded; to the
right of the drawing, first in Greek,
then in English: YOU HAVE KILLED,
O DANAOI, THE MOST LEARNED
WHO EVER CAUSED GREIF: THE
NIGHTENGALE OF THE MUSES,
THE VERY BEST OF THE GREEKS

The Sacred Way. We began
our ascent of the Sacred Way,
a letter "s" in reverse, ascending
the slope. We prepared to ascend
(we entered in); we found our
guide. *On entering the precinct*
you see [you do not see] *a bronze*
bull made by Theopropus, an
Aeginetan, and dedicated by the
Corcyraeans. It is said that in
Corcyra a bull used to leave the
herd and the pasture to go down and bellow by the sea-shore. The same thing happened every day, till the herdsman went down to the shore and beheld a countless shoal of tunnies. He told the Corcyraeans in the city, and they, after labouring in vain to catch them, sent envoys to Delphi, and in consequence they sacrificed the bull to Poseidon, and immediately after the sacrifice they caught the fish; and with the tithe of their take they dedicated the offerings at Olympia and Delphi.

: the gnomon is all
that remains

We were under a cliff. On the Sacred Way. The sloping
pathway, under a cliff. Meggie would take no pictures.
She wanted, first, her own silence, against the silence
of the cliff, as if even the sound of her camera might
snap that spur of Mt.
Parnassus down upon us,
that story, of Earth,
of Gaia, and her sacred
spring, and its guardian
serpent, and Apollo, the
new god, killing the
serpent, killing his way
into mercy, there, under
his temple

(we were climbing toward
his temple; we stopped to
stare at the Treasury of
the Athenians; we stopped
to catch our breath)

the dark and underworld
force of the earth,
struck into a speaking
splendour, into a prophetic,
a singing, splendour

persons
guilty of
sacrilege
were

flung

down the
(above)

cliff

(Jack and
Jill went
(quite a tumble

into the
Arkoudorema
(the Bear's
Gully

(belly)

After the hard questions we ask the question, What? What did you say? And the wind blowing. And how the wind came up, and the dust, I don't know. The wind was blowing. The feet of the tourists powered the dust. What was it I said I said? I said to Laura.

the

belly

button

of the world

where two eagles

flying from the world's ends

met

(meet?)

Pausanias: *What the Delphians call the Navel* (omphalos) *is made of white marble, and is said by them to be at the centre of the whole earth, and Pindar in one of his odes agrees with them.*

Meggie was taking pictures. Laura and I stood behind the omphalos and Meggie took a picture. Meggie and Laura stood behind the omphalos and I took a picture. Meggie and I stood behind the omphalos and Laura took a picture.

How does one pose for a picture taken at the belly button of the earth? What smile is not a smile of embarrassment? of self-satisfaction? of hybris? What angle of the arm does not betray a certain inappropriate possessiveness?

Frazer: *Even in his best days he* [Apollo] *did not always rise to verse, and in Plutarch's time the god appears to have given up the attempt in despair and to have generally confined himself to plain, if not lucid, prose.*

karpouzi:
watermelon

Only then did we realize,
we had lost our tour.

The Delphic letter E, cut into stone;
that is the mystery that no one can explain.

One day, one night, before Pausanias, before Socrates,
before Apollo (?)

the last person who knew what it means (what it meant)
perished.

That's the way it is.
The answer (or was it the question?):

mislaid?
stolen?
revised?
erased?
forgotten?
denied?
concealed?
replaced?
remembered?
laughed out
of court?
supposed
to be
sacrilegious?

watermelon is (not)
karpouzi

We went up the stone ramp, Laura and Meg and I. The floor, open to the sky, was as bare as a granary floor in summer before harvest begins. Six pillars remain where Croesus, told that in waging a war against a great power he would destroy a great power, heard, but did not understand.

They say that the most ancient temple of Apollo was made of laurel, and that the boughs were brought from the laurel in Tempe. The temple must have been in the shape of a shanty. The Delphians say that the second temple was made by bees out of wax and feathers, and that it was sent to the Hyperboreans by Apollo ... As to the story that they made a temple out of the fern that grows on the mountains by twinning the stalks together while they were still fresh and green, I do not admit it for a moment. Touching the third temple, it is no marvel that it was made of bronze, since Acrisius made a bronze chamber for his daughter ...

The wind was a dry wind.
There might have been
no sea at all, far below,
where the Pleistos River
winds its way through the
silver-green of olive
groves, out to blue
water. The dust was a
tight and grainy dust.

Frazer: "*a golden tripod resting on a bronze serpent* etc."
A base which is believed to have supported this famous
trophy has been found by the French at the highest part of
the Sacred Way, to the east of the temple of Apollo … The
bronze serpent on which the tripod rested is still to be
seen in the Almeidan, *the*
ancient Hippodrome, at
Constantinople, wither it
was transferred by
Constantine. The monument
consists really, not of a
single bronze serpent, but
of three such serpents so
skillfully intertwined that
their bodies appear as a
single spiral column, and
a very attentive
examination is necessary
to convince an observer
that there were actually
three serpents, not one.

after I saw Apollo's temple I
wanted to turn back; I wanted
to turn down the hill again,
down the long (the sacred)
way; it was Meg who insisted
we climb on higher: it was
her idea, there in the dust; in
the pine forest, the cicadas:
Meg said, let's climb up
higher, past the theatre (she,
pointing at the map in Laura's
book); and up we climbed,
higher, against the slope of
the mountain

"The Eggplant Poems," I
said, is a poem for which
we have no reliable text.
In fact, I haven't quite,
you might say, wrapped it
up. You mean, it doesn't
exist, Laura said. Now
wait a minute, I said. Is
there a difference between
a Greek poem which is lost
and a poem of mine which I
haven't been able to, for
whatever reasons, complete?
Yes, Laura said. Yes, Meggie said. We have references to
the lost Greek poem, I presume, Laura said, or we wouldn't
know it once existed. True, I said. True enough. But I
can tell you about "The Eggplant Poems." The eggplant, I
might add, is closely allied to the potato. Both belong to
the nightshade family. As for the poem itself…

I had missed the moment; the voice spoke and I was not
quite ready for my own hearing. I heard only the wind.
I was tired from the climbing, dusty, trying there to follow
after my young daughters. They leapt up the steep path.

The blown dust had closed my eyes. The cicadas were loud
in the pines. The pines smelled of their own sweating.
What I heard was a smaller sound, in the wind itself,
under the pulsing rhythm of the cicadas.

(The lost poem, *Margites.*
Homer's lost, satirical
epic, that comic poem
with a fool for its hero.
That lost poem that
might have changed
the warring world.)

(Sometimes,
high on a mountain,
one hears the lost poem.)

The voice reminded
me that it
had spoken. I
had heard it
there on the
temple floor while
I waited for Meg to take
a picture. She
and Laura, together,
were studying the
(almost) vanished treasuries,
the Rock of
Sibyl. I had
noticed the olive
groves, on the
plain of Itea,
far below.

There is a rock rising above the ground. The Delphians say
that on this rock Herophile, surnamed Sibyl, used to stand
and chant her oracles … The earlier Sibyl belonged, I
find, to the most ancient times. She is said by the Greeks

the mind
does not rhyme
with the hot wind;
beware
any trick of
the eye.

Autobiographillyria.
That's a new word.

to have been a daughter of Zeus
and Lamia, daughter of Poseidon,
and to have been the first woman
who chanted oracles; and they
say that she was named Sibyl by
the Libyans. Herophile was
younger, but still even she is
known to have been born before
the Trojan war; and she foretold
in her oracles that Helen would
grow up at Sparta to be the bane
of Asia and Europe, and that Ilium would be taken by the
Greeks on her account. The Delians remember a hymn which
she composed on Apollo … also she says sometimes that
she is Apollo's wedded wife, sometimes that she is his sister,
or again his daughter. These poetical statements she made
under the influence of frenzy and the inspiration of the god.

The cicadas in those pines. My daughters ahead of me. They had already found the stadium, the *stadion* that I had insisted was somewhere else, in my misreading of their map. They were ahead of me, farther up the mountain, out of sight.

this is what it is
to love daughters;
the cicadas sing;
the pine trees smell
of the green smell
of pine;
the tourists clamber
against the heat;
the steep trail opens
into the stone-edged
place where
horses ran

We had
passed the
temple, the
theatre too
below us;
I had
no interest
in the
stadium, the
sacred games,
the lost
sound of
colliding chariots,
the blunt
wreckage of
so many
dreams, the
bones discovering
mortality.

I was surprised at my own answer when my daughters asked me what I had asked. They knew I had fallen behind to get on with my listening. Or should I say, my questioning? They, somehow, knew that. I was surprised when I offered my explanation. I didn't have a chance, I said. My father asked the question first.

What are you doing here?
my father said.
Did I teach you nothing?

It was his awkward stating
(his farmer's patient
voice)
of the wind's ecstasy.

It was the tripod
raised to the stars.

It was the long trip
rewarded and
recalled.

It was the guidebook
lost.

The smell of blood
in the dusty air.

And the last, high
scream
of the sacrificed
beast.

Only my two daughters, smiling in their sceptical delight:
their father had heard the oracle speak. They were so
pleased with me, already I was a story to tell their friends.
We sat down on the stone seats, in the stadium. I wanted to
rest. Do you know what? they would begin, they were
already beginning, to their smiling, amused, delighted
friends. Do you know what happened …

And I, not leading, following after my tall, blonde daughters,
there in the hot Greek sun of that August day, I had heard
the speaking in the wind.

What are you doing here?
Did I teach you nothing?

Let's miss the bus, they said, my daughters. Let's stay.
We can get back, somehow, to Athens. They wanted to stay,
there in Delphi. The small hotels around the mountain's
corner. We had noticed them. The tavernas, promising a
night of wine.

(The poet, strayed.
The lost poem that
had to be lost, or
the world with it.

(The rippled water
rocks the moon.

(A penny, like the sun,
seen from a certain angle
surely is round.

It was I who said, We've got to go.

They wanted to stay, my two daughters. The sun came
down from the tall cliff. We had not even been inside the
museum.

It was I who said, We've got to go.

Keyed In

Consider this key I keep on my key chain.
I can't remember what door it opened.
I can't discard the key.

Maybe it opened the door to the cupboard
in which I kept my life story.
Where did that cupboard get to?

Maybe it fit the door of that old Chev
I drove away in when I left home.
Why didn't I keep a key to the house?

But maybe it is a key to the house.
Too bad the house is gone.
It's still the place where I live.

Sketches of a Lemon

1.

A lemon is almost round.
Some lemons are almost round.
A lemon is not round.

So much for that.

How can one argue that a lemon
is truly a lemon,
if the question can be argued?

So much for that.

I said, to Smaro
(I was working on this poem),
Smaro, I called, is there
(she was in the kitchen)
a lemon in the fridge?
No, she said.

So much for that.

2.

As my father used to say,
well I'll be cow-kicked
by a mule.

He was especially fond of
lemon meringue pie.

3.

I went and looked at Francis Ponge's poem
on blackberries. If blackberries can be
blackberries, I reasoned, by a kind of analogy,
lemons can, I would suppose, be lemons.

Such was not the case.

4.

Sketches, I remind myself,
not of a pear,
nor of an apple,
nor of a peach,
nor of a banana
(though the colour
raises questions),
nor of a nectarine,
nor, for that matter,
of a pomegranate,
nor of three cherries,
their stems joined,
nor of a plum,
nor of an apricot,
nor of the usual
bunch of grapes,
fresh from the vine,
just harvested,
glistening with dew—

Smaro, I called,
I'm hungry.

5.

What about oranges?
At least an orange
looks like an orange.
In fact, most oranges
bear a remarkable resemblance
to oranges.

6.

Smaro is rolling a lemon on the breadboard.
The breadboard, flat, horizontal, is motionless.
The lemon rolls back and forth on the motionless surface.
Smaro's hand moves horizontally, back and forth,
over the rolling lemon.

One could draw a diagram of the three related objects,
deduce therefrom a number of mechanical principles.

7.

I had a very strong desire
to kiss a lemon.
No one was watching.
I kissed a lemon.

So much for that.

8.

I bought a second-hand car—
Okay, okay.

9.

If someone asked me,
how is a lemon shaped?

(the salmon
(the oven
(the lemon

I'd say a lemon is shaped
exactly like an hour.

(Now we're getting somewhere.)

10.

The lemon cure.
In each glass
mix: 1 stick cinnamon
1 teaspoon honey
2 cloves
2 jiggers rum
1/2 slice lemon
hot water to taste

Repeat as necessary.

11.

poem for a child who has just bit into
a halved lemon that has just been squeezed:

see, what did I tell you, see,
what did I tell you, see, what
did I tell you, see, what did
I tell you, see, what did I
tell you, see, what did I tell
you, see, what did I tell you,
see, what did I tell you, see,
what did I tell you, see, what
did I tell you, see, what did
I tell you, see, what did I
tell you, see, what did I tell
you, see, what did I tell you

One could, of course, go on.

12.

This hour is shaped like
a lemon. We taste its light

on the baked salmon.
The tree itself is elsewhere.

We make faces, liking the
sour surprise. Our teeth melt.

it is a matter of winter

We fly south to forget winter and instead
we remember the long color of snow.

We seek to recover the sun and instead
we imagine the uses of shade, carrying

our heads in shadows, our arms in
screening oils that prevent the light.

We are become old, we say, and embrace
the moment simply by lying down

on hot sand, our bare, unsalvaged bodies
ripening like wheat in northern fields.

We come here to loaf by water and read;
instead the words slash each solitude

into nakedness, and once again Iphigenia
becomes the shoreline sacrifice

so that the ships might sail to Troy,
and loss tear down the towers.

Stonehenge surely is a stone clock that begs,
Please, sun, come back from your far drowning.

The soldiers at Dieppe, again and again that August day,
wading ashore in the red waves, meet winter.

And so it goes. We who are bandaged lie bandaged
in our dreams. It is a matter of winter.

Here by the salt sea, we dare to hope by remembering:
salt eats the snow from the hidden road.

The Lost Narrative of Mrs. David Thompson (Edited by Robert Kroetsch)

for Dennis and Diane Cooley

1

The knife of his body opened me and then I became his wife.
The knife of his body emptied me and then he became my life.

2

I was fourteen. There was no preacher in the post on the Churchill River.
I was sixteen. Spring, 1801. There was no doctor to deliver our first child.

My name is Charlotte Small. I gave birth to thirteen of David's children,
seven sons and six daughters. David always said his evening prayers.

My mother was Cree. She refused to reveal her true name.
My father was Patrick Small, who had gone back without us to London.

David was the North West Company's best surveyor. The West is tangled.
A sheet of paper is neat. What do you decide to write down? I asked him.

3

David said there was wilderness all around us. Everywhere I looked
I saw food and shelter. Sometimes David's eyes were two beaver pelts.

I was quicker with a paddle than any of David's men.
Sometimes the water was my only mirror. I combed my hair.

Sometimes I found roots we could boil and eat to shame our hunger.
The loneliness of the hunter congeals the blood.

I write down the sun, he said. I write down the stars.
David, I said, you should write down the names of your children.

4

I had thought a surveyor would dream the short and the long
in patches of light, not in shades of conquest. I was wrong.

He so loved the strangers he thought he feared. The Kootanae. The Piegan.
They told him he could learn to dance; he borrowed a pair of snowshoes.

The trick was to find a pass through the Rockies. David embraced
tomorrow.
I rinsed the heart of a caribou, there at the toe of a glacier.

5

He wrote down each gift of tobacco, each count of animal skins.
He asked why I wrote down nothing.

I wore a necklace of porcupine quills. They were dyed the colours
of blood and sky. I'm not sure he ever noticed.

6

He was busy creating his map, my homely world become
his map's appetite, a matter of killing and cutting and sum.

Pleasure and pain, for him, were pretty much the same thing.
The trouble was, I could tell the difference. I could smell water.

He came with a subdued fury, exhaustion and desire in a dead heat.
He might have been finding the Columbia River's fabled source.

7

Athabasca. The canoemen, wading waist-deep, towing upstream
in the naked cold, swore the name. Athabasca, they said. To no one at all.

The trick was to find a pass through the Rockies. Ice is slow to bend.
I rinsed the heart of a caribou, there at the toe of a glacier.

8

He dreamed a passage. He dreamed a find and its fame.
He dreamed a mountain of beaver pelts.

He dreamed a family, the lost boy from London,
making a map, always, making his map of nowhere.

A sheet of paper is as big as the world.
A sheet of paper is less than the flight of a swallow.

There is no such thing as world, only the flash of salmon
in your Kootanae River. [Your crew was dying of hunger.]

9

How do you run away from home? Perhaps he was seeking his mother.
I loved him to our dying days. We slept beside running water.

Home is a hot bowl in the frost of dawn. Home is a tent peg.
Home is a man crying in his sleep. Home is the shadow of an owl.

10

You got to your undiscovered place and found whole tribes
encamped on the river's shore. You asked them not to tell.

You stumbled into the wisdom of coffins. You made your choice;
you measured yourself for death, you with your courage and arithmetic.

A cradleboard tight on my back, I counted life with footsteps.
The gnarled root carries the wind-ripped tree.

Ten Simple Questions for David Thompson (Recorded by Robert Kroetsch)

for David Staines

1 How come you didn't find us?
We were waiting there in the future. Waiting.

We were dressed as timber stands and gold deposits.
And grizzly bears. We called your name.

2 What did you use as a toothbrush? Check one or more: Magpie feathers.
Wool from a buffalo's hump. Sand from the Athabasca's headwaters.

You kept your teeth sharp. They were the colour of bleached beaver skulls.
Danger was cleansing. Some mornings the sun got caught in your teeth.

3 Where shall we say you have gone?
Canada Post is holding your mail.

VISA wonders why you haven't paid your bill.
They have people in India right this minute, working the phones.

4 Did you sleep in your moccasins? My wife wants to know.
She imagines each night that you were a passionate lover.

I tell her you smelled of tanned moosehide. Each night,
to my nightly surprise, that excites her. She kicks me out of bed.

5 What was the nature of space for you? In general, I mean.
Not when you were on horseback. Or in a canoe.

We all have dreams of not being able to move.
You invested distance with the appeal of the pornographic.

6 Did you feel that, on the whole, the market economy was good
to the inhabitants of the country? I'm not talking guns and whisky.

Rumour has it you died, there in Montréal,
near The Company's downtown office, not a penny to your name.

7 Where, on average, did you find beauty? As a boy
you played in Westminster Abbey, read *Gulliver's Travels*.

As a man you worked in the Rockies. You found, perchance,
the irresistible ache of rock, the charm of summer snow.

8 About your Great Map: what does your map map?
We've been using it to look for oil. Under the contours you measured.

The tailing ponds fool the ducks and the geese. They assume they can land,
feed, sleep, build nests, raise their young. We like to fly south in winter.

9 Who shall we say was here? People are inquiring.
Libraries are making astute investments. They think you were a book.

Just the other day officials named a highway in your name.
They think you were a road.

10 Did you pack a bottle of liniment in the bow of your canoe?
Advertisers are inquiring. Anything that might pass as a painkiller.

No more of that fur trade stuff. No more of that writing your travels.
You could make a fortune in sponsorships. Just give me a call.

Late April? 1991

please delete, where indicated

if I understand you correctly you are saying that you

catastrophe is a shade of blue. Or is it merely the name
of a perfume that once

the crispness of the celery, so to speak, somehow
reminded me

The distortion of the poem by the image is endemic
to analysis, or at least your analysis suggests

If your heart isn't in it, why eat the goulash, comma

perhaps the occasion will present itself later, just
as did the clay—was it tablets or feet?—of your

the title should have read, *Flight From Lisbon to
Madrid*, as you suggested on the phone, when you
phoned from Madrid to tell me about the nude photos
your new acquaintance

masquerade, not Methuselah

tenebrous and tenebrific are both perfectly good
words, darkly majestic, perhaps, even verging, perhaps,
on the pretentious, as you so aptly

the usual, a boiled egg, and, of all things, sourdough

cookbooks, not books, cookbooks.

please insert, where indicated

(becomes more and more—) another kettle of fish
entirely, your wishing, if it all possible,

not the usual usual, no, but not the unusual either.

or abundance or, for that matter, superfluity, or
whatever it will take to bust the

hang it on the line, hang it in the weather, enough
of this dryer set on gentle stuff, enough

(No eyebrows? You say he has *no* eyebrows?)

isotherms, or, having abandoned them too, any other
versions of order, the usual stays against chaos,
the usual lumpy porridge, the usual rubbing of knees
together under the laden table, the usual

and if, as you suggest in your last letter, we are at best
an activity, at worst

corn or asparagus tips, either, thank you. Creamed
beets make a nice vegetable, if only for the colour

Quick. Zoti.

poetry and potatoes certainly may appear in the same
sentence

April 29–May 4, 1991

please delete, where indicated

or metaphor, seeking stolid immunity
under the law of

You should design a candlestick for candles
that are to be burnt at both

we could buy a cow, then, rumination being what it is,

chloroform and love, in their dispensations

cauliflower comes to mind, the insides of an egg (roll),
the guts on a windshield, emphysema, hay fever

Melopeia, you may recall, is the word Ezra employs,
in his ABC

surely the invention of apple pie did much to undo
what we call

grammar itself serves you as a kind of jealous garment
that prevents me from touching your

please insert, where indicated

(I am tired of tracking my body.)

Hockey Night in Canaan. But you promised

the heart beware, said I, summing up and, generously,
subtracting (what I could).

or calibrate the garden with my knees, bend
slowly in, cry out and sigh

The finitude of never is a tough nut to crack.
I study the faces of stones. I dial direct
to darkness.

please plead, she said, joking as we closed our eyes
and jumped

like carbuncle, a word of ambiguous intention,
like like as in I like you

we could, you said, unfairly, I thought, use it as
a catapult.

or, again, if *your* heart isn't in it, said the cannibal
to the (blank?), why eat the goulash?

in its later stages the lover, like the dinosaur in
earlier times, not noticing the approach of the

November 9, 1983: For Robert Hilles

Just what the hell is a nature poem,
Robert? Here I am in Calgary to talk
a reading, six hours early, thanks (a lot)
to Air Canada's schedule. I have, in

the Holiday Inn on 8th, a room where
I could write a poem or have (or not) a
sexual fantasy, but instead I walk
the slick sidewalks, watching the snow

come down. It's hardly even snow. Well,
yes, it's snow all right, white enough.
The small flakes blur the tall buildings,
their walls reflect, you guessed it,

snow. Snow is the text, read it, poet.
Fat chance. The air is full
of musical notes. White notes, that is.
They melt to grey on my glasses. I can

hardly read. The sidewalk is slick.
The molten towers, high on the season's
first snow, sway around me. I'm almost
shy. But then I begin to join the dance.

Nation in Peril

BANFF ELK GIVES BIRTH TO TOURIST
SUSPECT IN HAND
[SWM, 51. animal lover, likes long walks…]

FINDS LIVE DRAGON IN CEREAL BOX
CUSTOMER DEMANDS REFUND
[SWM, 37, vegan, likes to eat out…]

CANADIAN MALE FAKES ORGASM
WOMEN CLAIM VIOLATION OF RIGHTS
[DWF, 46, professor, likes a good time…]

TORY MP SUPPORTS ARTS
RCMP LAY CHARGES
[SWF. 29, artist, will arrange private showing…]

Sub-text

Don’t look now but
I think we’re being followed.
The shadows fastened to our heels
are empty, deep, dark. Inviting.

[hornbook #99]

> The question is always a question of trace.
> What remains of what does not remain?

The unpublished Hornbook #99 may have occasioned, I would like to conjecture, Rita Kleinhart's refusal, for the final year of her life (if we are to believe that she is dead), to add further to the astonishing series initiated by poems #1 to #98.

She disappeared on June 26, 1992, at the age of fifty-five. A recluse by nature, she apparently traveled outside Canada only once; she gave only three public readings; she lectured twice to academic audiences. And of course she published the ninety-eight brief poems (all of them written between June 1987 and the spring of 1991, if my intuitions are correct) that are the basis of her quiet yet enduring reputation.

Kleinhart was invited, during the late spring of 1992, to visit Germany and lecture briefly to the Canadianists at Trier University. On her way back from Trier she paid a visit to the Museum of Modern Art in Frankfurt and while at the museum mailed a number of postcards to friends. She was not seen alive thereafter.

Her ranch in Central Alberta—her house overlooking the coulees and the valley of the Battle River—contained at the time of her disappearance neat stacks of scrawled notes, manuscripts, partially filled notebooks and, yes, unfinished (or unfinishable?) poems.

The opening of #99 exists in a number of versions, with no particular version indicated as her final choice. On the top of a sheaf of drafts I found two lines on a single sheet of paper:

> I am watching the weather channel.
> It is that kind of day.

Rita questioned and even rejected ideas of evolutionary
development in art. She had other fish to fry.

[hornbook #84]

Why don't you close doors? Rita once asked me, when I indiscreetly left a door open behind us. I was born on a raft, I replied.

I knew how to irk her and at times couldn't resist. Rita Kleinhart was persuaded that her notion of collective biography—the expression is mine, not hers—could not be located in a system of beliefs or a narrative of origins. It could only be located, literally and momentarily, in back doors.

Her fascination with back doors—of houses, of apartments, even of garages and barns and public buildings—announces her interest in collective biography. Her brief but eloquent poems on the subject of the back door speak to and of the pathetic beauty that we create by way of rejection and something that one might call denial. Back doors are, she proposes in her notebooks, the escape from transcendence. They are also the escape from so-called good neighbors and possibly from language itself.

I tell you this because my own recollections, along with the neat stacks of paper of which I have made mention, give the lie to the published poems so treasured by Kleinhart's (albeit too few) devoted readers.

[hornbook #61]

Rita Kleinhart was at work on a huge—and I would say, bizarre—work that ultimately, I am persuaded, caused her disappearance. She held to the conviction that she might so write her poems that she would leave each object or place or person that fell under her attention undisturbed.

Granted, she did not, looking at back doors, tug at latches or twist at knobs. And yet she proposed at one point in one of her notes (though she may have later abandoned the idea) that she would limit her investigation to her own township. A township is, of course, in its own insistent way, a box. Kleinhart has nothing to say on this matter. Or, at most, she drew on a sheet of paper a square full of squares, then commented in the margin: A township is not a box.

I might explain to the unwary reader that a township, as conceived in Kleinhart's home province, is a square of land measuring six miles by six miles, resulting in a grid made up of thirty-six squares of land each measuring one mile by one mile. These thirty-six sections (as they are called) are numbered from one to thirty-six, beginning not from the top left-hand corner as one might expect, but rather from the lower right-hand corner, then to the left, then up a row and to the right, then up a row and to the left, then up a row and to the right, in the time-honored manner of a farmer plowing a field with oxen or even a four-horse team.

Rita Kleinhart went too far, I feel, both with her notions of the nondevelopmental nature of the individual artist's work and with her commitment to versions of the serial.

Things happen, she writes, and then things happen. And there is sweet fuck all else to it.

[hornbook #4]

The hornbook is itself a book, but a book one page in length. Framed and wearing a handle, covered in transparent horn, it sets out to fool no one. It says its say. Rita Kleinhart seems not to have got a handle on this realization. What she claimed for her poems was exactly that which they did not provide: the clarity of the exact and solitary and visible page. The framed truth, present and unadorned. Not a page for the turning, no, but rather the poem as relentless as a mirror held in the hand.

The framed and confident statement, announcing precept or command; the framed list, offering the barest alphabet and numerals of our lives. A one-page book covered in horn, but not a horny book. The dehorned beast, offering its last sign and protection to protect the isolate sheet of paper and its insistent economy of words.

[hornbook #44]

[an endnote to begin with: Rita felt little need to travel in this ravaged world. She once heard me speak of the city of Coimbra in Portugal and (if I am not mistaken) wrote Hornbook #44 in response to my claiming to have shed tears at the sound of a voice I heard without ever laying eyes on the singer.]

1

I am happy in the Coimbra night.
The stars feed on the carrion of our lives.
There where the mountains break and fall
the city dreams a fatal song.

2

The castle at the end of the curled road
sings fado. The pale trees weep leaves,
offering embrace to stone.
I become the voice I hear.

3

The lemon tree by the window wears
two birds. The birds are not singing.
I listen to their song.
Why is the fountain crying?

4

The woman in the bus who sang
sang softly of our long delay.
We were going nowhere.
I drank the song the woman sang.

5

You were as strange as love.
The fado bar was empty,
except for all of us.
There in Coimbra, I listen.

[I hardly need to explain that Rita here misrepresents me badly. (Not to mention her inability to live in either the present or the past.) I had delivered a package of documents to a wine merchant in Oporto and while there decided I would take the train south to Coimbra, largely because I was told of a shop that had on sale some rare green tiles. It was not my intention to listen in on any fado. I might add that by the time I got to the tile shop the objects of my little quest were gone.]

[hornbook for a young poet]

Have bacon (four strips,
preferably) and eggs (two, sunnyside up),

hash browns with ketchup,
toast (white) with real strawberry jam,

a glass of orange juice (small will do),
and three cups of black coffee;

then mark one of the following
(please, not with an X):

a) Tune-up and body-tone clinics are available
at reasonable prices.

b) We do have to believe in something
(don't we?).

c) We proceed by heresies, yet intend
to get to where we are going.

d) Appetite will be the end of us.

[the inspiration hornbook]

You of the almighty zap,
Zeusifer, loose and zany,
let me sizzle on your throne
for maybe forty-eight seconds;
I've had enough of your poetry crap,
just give me the last word of this poem.

Man in the Moon

Man in the moon—
stars for supper,
hunger all day.

I'm Getting Old Now

I'm getting old now, I can tell. I dream
a lot of my mother. In my dream last night
she was in the garden, over the hill,
behind our house. She was standing. I was

playing in the pea vines. We were both happy.
Neither of us would move, in the dream. Perhaps
I wasn't playing. I was kneeling to pick peas.
My mother held in her apron the peas

we had picked together. She was standing still.
I knew she was watching me. She was
watching me grow. Like a bad weed, she liked
to say. That pleased her.

I'm getting old now. I wouldn't say I'm happy.
Serene is an adequate word. Death is not quite
the enemy it was. It is a kind of watching.

Death begins to seem a friend that one has almost
forgotten, then remembers again. In my dream,
last night, I was playing in the garden.

Sounding the Name

In this poem my mother is not dead.
The phone does not ring that October
morning of my fourteenth year.
The anonymous voice on the phone

does not say, Call Arthur to the phone.
Our hired man, a neighbour's son, quiet,
unpretentious, a man from the river hills
near our farm, does not turn from the phone,

he does not say, seeming to stress the time,
Your mother died at ten o'clock. My sister and I
do not look at each other, do not smile,
assuring each other (forever) that words are
pretenders.

In this poem my mother is not dead,
she is in the kitchen, finishing the October
canning. I am helping in the kitchen.

I wash the cucumbers. My mother asks me
to go pick some dill. The ducks are migrating.
I forget to close the garden gate.

Sonnet #5

nothing

but

nothing
but
darkness
outside my
window

the shape of
water

nothing
but

darkness

outside

my window

nothing but
darkness

Afterword

#An afterword in which a reader tries to encapsulate the writing of Robert Kroetsch, silent poet (in homage to *Alibi*, which claims to be fiction rather than poetry)

> What after all is a poem
> but a longing for a possible
> reality? ("[the melancholia hornbook]" *The Hornbooks of Rita K* 95)

Robert Kroetsch declared, often, that he was giving up poetry. Then he would declare that he was giving up fiction. Then he would admit that he was secretly writing a few poems, here and there. And had finished a novel, and an essay. Clearly more interested in denial than admission, he would occasionally confess to being a poet, although in one poem, after having been kicked off a bucking bull, he says that he is "going to be a writer" (*A Likely Story* 113). And he was certainly that. Choosing a selection of Kroetsch's poems from his miscellaneous and wide-ranging oeuvre is a task both mammoth and daunting. David Eso's intrepid and impeccable curation here dares to announce both pleasure and trepidation, reminding the reader of Kroetsch's own words in "The Ledger,"

> Men felt terror.
> They proposed. (*Completed Field Notes* 23)

In proposing this selection, David Eso most certainly felt terror, but delight as well. While "terror of women" was a thread in Kroetsch's writing, it was also a trope that hid his deeper terror, of any conclusion or finality. There is no complete collected poetry of Robert Kroetsch. The published work and the scattered fragments and chapbooks ("what remains of what does not remain" "[hornbook#99]") declare even more fragments, all of them slowly erasing their cohesion and potential closure.

No one was prepared for Robert Kroetsch's death in an automobile accident in June of 2011. For all that he was aging (he had passed 80), had been diagnosed with Parkinson's disease (remarkable only by a slight tremor), and that he brandished a metallic-blue cane, Robert Kroetsch belonged to the realm of those paradoxically ageless. His energies as pyrotechnical as ever, his engagement with words and language entire, he managed a culmination of creative trickster, brilliant rogue, and wise sage. Although he harboured a substratum of melancholia, advancing years and their inscription on his body seemed to free him from expectation and confinement. He was wildly inventive in his stories and poems, passionate in his recollections, and persistently writing.

Robert Kroetsch returned to Alberta in 2009 to practise, he told me, "getting old," determined, he claimed, "to get braced for old age." He had travelled a protean circle in his life, from the Battle River country in central Alberta to the University of Alberta in Edmonton, to the riverboats on the Mackenzie, to Goose Bay, Labrador, and then to universities in Montreal, Vermont, and Iowa, before teaching for thirteen years at the State University of New York in Binghamton. He returned to Canada, served as writer-in-residence in Winnipeg, Calgary, and Lethbridge, and then as a professor at the University of Manitoba. After some years he moved to Victoria, then back to Manitoba, and finally back to Alberta. Despite his restlessness, beautifully detailed by Dennis Cooley in *The Home Place*, he exerted a profound intellectual impact, his connection to the literary world especially powerful; and he was a friend, teacher, or mentor to hundreds of young and old Canadian writers, more influential than his reputation measures.

His decision to return to Alberta was almost covert. He wrote to me, "Aritha, I'm in Leduc, getting ready to move into a seniors' residence and give it a summer try. More soon as sanity sets in. Robert" (personal email, 30 April 2009). Leduc is the kind of town where Kroetsch felt at home, not too large but large enough, retaining a rural spirit despite being an industrial support centre close to the Edmonton airport. There he found an ice-cream shop (a necessity for him), a good Italian restaurant, an excellent Indian restaurant, he played cards with his sisters, and, as he said, "began to practice up" for death. That last was not at all predictable, but he seemed to relish every moment he experienced as if it might be his last. Kroetsch's oeuvre, his many novels and essays and poems, the chorus of words in his endlessly incomplete *Completed Field Notes*, demonstrate a prescience unusual in the flotsam left by literary figures. While he was adamantly voracious in his passion for life and avoided any mention of death (I gave him Julian Barnes's book *Nothing to Be Frightened Of* and he refused to read it), he seemed also uncannily prepared for the next move, double or nothing. He was a restless figure, his movement resisting stasis, persistently unwilling to "stay put." In *The Home Place*, Dennis Cooley highlights his "perpetual flight" (9), how in one year he took seventy-five flights. We might not blink at that vagabondage now, but in 1976 it comprised an outrageous amount of travel. Surprisingly, then, Kroetsch was also, in his yearning for some "dream of origins," nostalgic, in the best sense of that word. His journeys outward bolstered always a determination to return—where? Home, to some source, some wellspring. He evaded absence by evading absence and, inevitably lonesome, travelled to chase his own homesickness.

#the academic, aka intellectual bullshit

Robert Kroetsch's work was not popular. His writing puzzled people, chagrined them, made them doubt their own understanding. The coy and moralizing were outraged by his blunt carnality, his *recherché* rurality. The sophisticated were surprised by his ribaldry, and worried about missing his meaning. His depictions of academics and archivists, of professors and graduate students (there are a surprising number of graduate student characters with unfinished theses in Kroetsch's work, hardly biographical because he finished his, although he knew many struggling graduate students and was always encouraging them), could be acerbic, and he strips the learned and the pretentious down to their skins, even while he is the most cerebral of writers himself. His writing not only measured a fissure in Canadian literature, but activated postmodern influences, beautifully unpacked in Linda Hutcheon's still pivotal essay on him as "the master of paradoxes" (161). He revelled in the influences of Derrida, Heidegger, and Foucault, documented in detail in *Labyrinths of Voice: Conversations with Robert Kroetsch* (1982). His life's work demonstrated an unusual conundrum, that of creative critic and critically conscious artist. Hutcheon correctly identifies his primary impetus as a "merging of the theoretical and the literary" (161); he reads and writes with an ambivalence that subverts genre, and he considers critique a creative exercise: "criticism is really a version of story, you see; I think we are telling the story to each other of how we get at story. It is the story of our search for story. That's why criticism is *so* exciting. Not because it provides answers, but because it is a version of story" (*Labyrinths* 30). He could have elaborated that contention to note that criticism is also a version of poetry, or simply a version of version.

#on nakedness

The enigmatic sparseness of Robert Kroetsch's writing suggests an implicit *in flagrante*; and the very directness of his syntax belies the complex content. He does not skirt or over-modify; he employs metaphor and simile sparingly. In the short poem "hornbook #73," he declares:

> When I tell you
> that I love you
> I am trying to tell you
> that I love you. (*Hornbooks* 97)

The best of arguments against interpretation, it achieves an intensity missing in most "love" poems that rely on comparison. Language is what language is, and can perform only its own performance. The vividness attached to that insistence then doubles back on its ulterior motive, and the reader is compelled to puzzle over its axiomatic determination. In "[hornbook C]" the persona actually reaches for a metaphor:

> This is a shaky proposition, but: let's give it a try: Poetry
> is a changing of the light (*Hornbooks* 84)

The very deliberation of the two colons, one following the other, performs doubt, the "shaky proposition" upheld by the image of time and its constant intervention with expression. The poet becomes apostate, the doubting poet wanting to put his fingers in the wound of his profession and its desires. Readers tend to hesitate, dubious about intent, but searching for broader or deeper or secret meanings inevitably leads to a cul-de-sac. "Sketches of a Lemon," in its performance as a *dinggedict*, insists on this tautology.

How can one argue that a lemon
is truly a lemon,
if the question can be argued? (*Completed Field Notes* 76)

How does this figure of speech bypass the conundrum of any *tertium comparationis*? Not quite a palindromic sentence, but intricately related to the matryoshka principle, every line in this poem suggests its own *mise en abyme.* Kroetsch would doubtless prefer onion routing, where peeling off the outer layer reveals a similar onion within; I tend to favour the Droste effect, the recursive effigy of the Dutch nurse holding a tray with the hot chocolate cup and a tin of Droste chocolate bearing a smaller image of her holding the same object, which in turn bears a smaller image of her holding the same object, and so on and so on. What we imagine to be the essence or the telling takes on, in Kroetsch's constant play with how words can surprise themselves, a new dimension, simpler but also more intricate. And he seizes every opportunity for digression, exploring how to balance a conundrum on the edge of a knife and still make a riddle shine with transparency.

#escaping form; or #adding up

Kroetsch's poetry deploys columns, notations, citations, lists, and sequences, and his fascination with collection persists as accrual, reckoning, and enumeration. He reframes too the structures of poetry, calling poems that are not sonnets sonnets, interspersing diaries and lyrics with narrative, interrupting excerpts with litany and commentary, alluding to multiple forms without ever exercising their formalism. Like the watch the persona takes apart in the poem "Lonesome Writer Diptych" (*A Likely Story* 110), Kroetsch dismantles and then, puzzled at the pieces on the table in front of him, tries to get a poem "back together," reassembling and creating a new instrument. This medley of aggregation and jumble echoes his persistent question "Why is every poem a study in its own repetitions?" (*Hornbooks* 94). The last section of that collection, entitled "The Red Shale Hornbooks," leans on shale's characteristic fissility, its mixture of fragments and particles. His long poem *"field notes"* (which he likened to the notes "kept by the archaeologist") (*Lovely Treachery* 129) marks his interest in accretion rather than conclusion, his suspicion of unity. "The problem for the writer of the contemporary long poem is to honour our disbelief in belief—that is, to recognize and explore our distrust of system, of grid, of monisms, of cosmologies . . . —and at the same time write a long work that has some kind of (under erasure) unity" (*Lovely* 118). Readers may seek to find a pattern or a grid, but his continuing poem, his long and yet too-short poem, dances all over the page, digresses, detours, and then gathers disparate approaches together into a unique abridgement. Naming, the shape of naming, the attraction of names, the allure of onomasty, recurs too. Kroetsch names names. He names his friends and enemies. He names the many places that he visited and the places he called home. He names naming and unnaming until he reaches the veritable impasse of naming death, his last collection, *Too Bad*, a cumulative anti-sonnet about absence and its most terrible naming, loss.

#digression to place and character

Critics compete to identify Robert Kroetsch's most enigmatic work, often ignoring the place-lineaments that structure his writing, giving it a shape that form does not. In his most potent poem, "The Frankfurt *Hauptbahnhof*" (not included here, for it is much anthologized), the poet addresses a moment of confusion in that railway station (one of the largest in Europe) in Frankfurt in 1983, when he meets his double and discovers himself as "the gone stranger" (*Completed Field Notes* 193). His epiphany's orientation throws into relief the many locations Kroetsch scouts, from Rome to Salonika, from China to Portugal. Troy, Stonehenge, the Acropolis, the Parthenon, and Coimbra transport what is ancient into the present, and collapse the two. "Delphi: Commentary" combines the routine of travel with translations, allusions, citations, and even a collision of alphabets, to the moment when the persona poses a question to the oracle, who does not answer, but instead asks a question in return, in the voice of Kroetsch's father:

> What are you doing here? . . .
> Did I teach you nothing? (*Completed* 187)

The incredulity of these questions and these many peregrinations are digressions toward home, as Dennis Cooley so perceptively articulates, governing Kroetsch's "acute sense of the lost home" (*Home* 7) as a perpetually homesick writer who sought always to re-hear the rhythms of the speech of his childhood.

#raging against death and time

The final words of Kroetsch's last published novel are "Even a long life is short. We must learn to hold each other" (*Man from the Creeks* 334).

Those were the last words we exchanged when I dropped Robert Kroetsch off in Canmore, Alberta, on Tuesday, June 14, 2011.

"Even a long life is short," he said.

"Have fun," I told him. "See you in a couple of weeks."

The young, unspeakably fit men representing Canmore's ArtsPeak Festival, Dave Eso and Chris Masson, promised him that they were going to get him to climb a mountain. He swung his cane and laughed, jauntily climbed the stairs of the condo.

#holding, or advice to friends

For all its cerebral bent, its back-and-forth hesitancy, Kroetsch's poetry shines with warmth and intimacy, and while refusing flourishes or instruction, ultimately reveals most a desire for connection, two persons with a holding preposition. In *What the Crow Said,* Liebhaber composes a perfect novel, one sentence long, "a novel that anyone could memorize. *You in my arms*" (*Crow* 146). The perfect, yearning destination, the love poem/novel holds two characters, two bodies, arms and desire and fulfillment in four words.

#but we were talking about death

Most striking in Kroetsch's poetry is its search for both long life and answers, even while discomfort locates his poetry's situation and sensation. His many personae feel relieved when they are made to suffer, just a bit. And while he adamantly pretends that he and death have no connection, death trespasses all his poetry in its seeking answers, the Delphi oracle, the father lonesome for death, the poems grieving his mother and sister. The poetry revels in accidents, deaths as brusque and violent and surprising as the lives of those who lose them, echoing both the title of his last collection, *Too Bad,* and his own death, with and without irony.

A European scholar and I set off on a research trip, to visit Heisler, just north of the Battle River in Alberta, and to see the inspiration for so much of Kroetsch's energy. We did not find the Wanda church, but we found what might have been the Wanda school, one of those abandoned schoolhouses built so optimistically by early settlers, eager that their children be subject to literacy. We decided (as researchers are wont to do, whatever the evidence) that Kroetsch must have gone there. The schoolhouse was in ruins, dishevelled, windows broken, birds nesting, the roof rotting. Tramps and teenagers had certainly used it for sleeping and drinking and frightening one another. But sprayed on one wall, in large blurred letters, was written, "Forgive me, please."

Only a few messages come to us from beyond the grave.

Kroetsch concealed his perplexity within pages of fiction and poetry and non-fiction, leaving it to us to decipher and puzzle out his insight and his prophecy. His intricate legacy is what we have, and where readers can find pleasure and wisdom. In "Sounding the Name," in a poem called "I'm Getting Old Now," he writes:

> I'm getting old now. I wouldn't say I'm happy.
> Serene is an adequate word. Death is not quite
> the enemy it was. It is a kind of watching. (*Completed* 202)

He watched the world, "watching" a repeated action in his work. He watched snow and the Weather Channel, and he watched for a coming spring. He evaded absence by evading absence and, inevitably lonesome for home, became the man in the corner of the world, watching the action.

> We silence words
> by writing them down (42)

Best of all, he invented a garden, and then set out to write it.

—Aritha van Herk

Works Cited

Barnes, Julian. *Nothing to Be Frightened Of.* London: Jonathon Cape, 2008.

Cooley, Dennis. *The Home Place.* Edmonton: University of Alberta Press, 2018

Hutcheon, Linda. "Seeing Double: Concluding with Kroetsch." *The Canadian Postmodern.* Toronto: Oxford University Press, 1988.

Kroetsch, Robert. *Completed Field Notes.* Edmonton: University of Alberta Press, 2000.

———. *The Hornbooks of Rita K.* Edmonton: University of Alberta Press, 2001.

———. *A Likely Story: The Writing Life.* Red Deer: Red Deer College Press, 1995.

———. *The Lovely Treachery of Words: Essays Selected and New.* Toronto: Oxford University Press, 1989.

———. *The Man from the Creeks.* Toronto: Random House, 1998.

———. *Too Bad: Sketches Toward a Self-Portrait.* Edmonton: University of Alberta Press, 2010.

———. *What the Crow Said.* Edmonton: University of Alberta Press, 1998.

Neuman, Shirley and Robert Wilson. *Labyrinths of Voice: Conversations with Robert Kroetsch.* Edmonton: NeWest Press, 1982.

Further Reading

Readers who seek an immersive encounter with Kroetsch's poetry should first access *Completed Field Notes* (first published in 1989, reprinted in 2000), along with other volumes drawn on here.

Kroetsch's novels, like his poems, are often comic. Subsequent to *But We Are Exiles* (1965) and *The Words of My Roaring* (1966), *The Studhorse Man* (1969) won the Governor General's Literary Award. *Gone Indian* (1973), *Badlands* (1975), *What the Crow Said* (1978), and *Alibi* (1984) are sprawling, multi-voiced, and often grotesquely funny. Many readers may find that the author pushed his experimental luck too far with *The Puppeteer* (1992). *The Man from the Creeks* (1998) builds a fictional Klondike based upon an intertext, the poem "The Shooting of Dan McGrew" by Robert Service.

Alongside poetry collections and novels, Kroetsch produced non-fiction titles. The travel book *Alberta* (1968) contributed to a series of Canadian writers exploring their home provinces. A selection of personal journals appeared as *The* Crow *Journals* (1980). Interviews and conversations were published as *Labyrinths of Voice* (1982) and *Abundance* (2007). His writerly memoir *A Likely Story* (1995) contains poetry as well. The best source for his literary theory and criticism, which often combines personal essay, is *The Lovely Treachery of Words* (1989). Kroetsch also edited and co-edited collections of creative and scholarly writing. Such titles include *Sundogs: Stories from Saskatchewan* (1980), *The Selected Poems of Douglas Barbour* (1985), and *Gaining Ground: European Critics on Canadian Literature* (1985).

Many scholars have contributed to Kroetsch's legacy. *Robert Kroetsch: Essays on his work*, edited by Nicole Markotić, gathers a range of voices. Aritha van Herk composed a "Biocritical Essay" to introduce the published finding aid to *The Robert Kroetsch Papers, First Accession* (1986). Dennis Cooley has published the only book-length study of Kroetsch as poet, *The Home Place* (2016). Linda Hutcheon discusses him in her concluding chapter to *The Canadian Postmodern* (1988). Simona Bertacco's *Out of Place* (2002) is useful on *boundary 2* and other topics.

A complete list of the author's publications is available through robertkroetsch.ca, a website maintained by executors for the author's estate.

Acknowledgements

All poems in this volume are reprinted by permission of the Robert Kroetsch Estate.

The University of Alberta Press has granted permission to reprint the following poems from their edition *Completed Field Notes* (2000): "Stone Hammer Poem," "Sketches of a Lemon," and (from *Advice for My Friends*) "Having a Word with Columbus ..." and "November 9, 1983 ..."; "Delphi Commentary"; "Sydney" and "Wellington, New Zealand," from *Spending the Morning on the Beach*; and "I'm Getting Old Now," "Sounding the Name," and "Sonnet #5," from *Sounding the Name*.

The University of Alberta Press has also granted permission to reprint the following: "Pirate Story," "Keyed In," "Taste," and "Nation in Peril," which are from Kroetsch's final poetry collection, *Too Bad: Sketches Toward a Self-Portrait* (2010); "Are we there yet?" and "it is a matter of winter," which come from *The Snow Bird Poems* (2004); and the hornbook suite of poems, which are from *The Horn Books of Rita K* (2001). The latter was shortlisted for the Governor General's Award for poetry. Smaro Kamboureli in her wisdom indicated why the hornbook poems deserved more space than originally allotted. The editor thanks her for that and other useful conversations during preparations for this book.

"Spring Harvest" and "Projected Visit" appeared in *The stone hammer poems, 1960–1975*, published by Oolichan Books, and are reprinted here by permission of the publisher.

Red Deer [College] Press published Kroetsch's writerly memoir *A Likely Story* in 1995; "Lonesome Writer Diptych" is reprinted from that volume with the publisher's permission.

Wrinkle Press has granted permission to reprint the *David Thompson* and *Mrs. David Thompson* chapbooks (2009). "Sub-text" is reprinted from the 2011 chapbook *Writer's Block* with permission from Greenboathouse press.

The following poems are reprinted by permission of the Robert Kroetsch Estate. "Tourist from Toronto" appeared in the journal *alphabet* in 1967. "There Is a World" is reprinted from the 1979 collection *Seed Catalogue* by Turnstone Press. "as the flowers see them" is apparently an unpublished poem, preserved in the Robert Kroetsch Papers (MsC 591/96.6 42.3). It appears alongside two other poems, seemingly unpublished as well: "shakeys" and "winter dark." *Revisions of Letters Already Sent* was issued in a run of 250 copies by disOrientation chapbooks of Calgary, Alberta—now defunct. A copy is preserved in the Robert Kroetsch Papers, University of Calgary, Special Collections, MsC 591/96.6 52.12. The first and second sequence from that publication are reprinted here: "Late April? 1991" and "April 29–May 4, 1991." "Man in the Moon" was composed during a haiku- and tanka-writing workshop hosted by David Eso. Kroetsch attended the workshop in conjunction with his prominent role in the 2011 ArtsPeak festival in Canmore, Alberta, at the age of eighty-four. Shortly thereafter, he died in an accident en route to Leduc, Alberta. The poem first appeared in *The Rocky Mountain Outlook* for 30 June 2011.

The editor thanks Laurie Ricou, Aritha van Herk, Iain Higgins, Eric Miller, David Staines, Neil Besner, Tristan Martel, Hilary McMahon, and the executors of Robert Kroetsch for their various supports. Thanks are also due to the Estate of artist John Snow, who generously allowed his *Prairie Cactus* to serve as the cover image for this volume. Kroetsch would likely have approved this choice, given that he collected prints by John Snow and that he spent time as resident writer at the John Snow House in Calgary.

lps Books in the Laurier Poetry Series
Published by Wilfrid Laurier University Press

Nelson Ball	*Certain Details: The Poetry of Nelson Ball*, selected with an introduction by Stuart Ross, with an afterword by Nelson Ball • 2016 • xxiv + 86 pp. • ISBN 978-1-77112-246-7
derek beaulieu	*Please, No More Poetry: The Poetry of derek beaulieu*, edited by Kit Dobson, with an afterword by Lori Emerson • 2013 • xvi + 74 pp. • ISBN 978-1-55458-829-9
Dionne Brand	*Fierce Departures: The Poetry of Dionne Brand*, edited by Leslie C. Sanders, with an afterword by Dionne Brand • 2009 • xvi + 44 pp. • ISBN 978-1-55458-038-5
Di Brandt	*Speaking of Power: The Poetry of Di Brandt*, edited by Tanis MacDonald, with an afterword by Di Brandt • 2006 • xvi + 56 pp. • ISBN 978-0-88920-506-2
Nicole Brossard	*Mobility of Light: The Poetry of Nicole Brossard*, edited by Louise H. Forsyth, with an afterword by Nicole Brossard • 2009 • xxvi + 118 pp. • ISBN 978-1-55458-047-7
Alice Burdick	*Deportment: The Poetry of Alice Burdick*, edited by Alessandro Porco • 2018 • xxx + 64 pp. • ISBN 978-1-77112-380-8
Margaret Christakos	*Space Between Her Lips: The Poetry of Margaret Christakos*, edited by Gregory Betts, with an afterword by Margaret Christakos • 2017 • xxviii + 68 pp. • ISBN 978-1-77112-297-9
George Elliott Clarke	*Blues and Bliss: The Poetry of George Elliott Clarke*, edited by Jon Paul Fiorentino, with an afterword by George Elliott Clarke • 2008 • xviii + 72 pp. • ISBN 978-1-55458-060-6
Dennis Cooley	*By Word of Mouth: The Poetry of Dennis Cooley*, edited by Nicole Markotić, with an afterword by Dennis Cooley • 2007 • xxii + 62 pp. • ISBN 978-1-55458-007-1
Lorna Crozier	*Before the First Word: The Poetry of Lorna Crozier*, edited by Catherine Hunter, with an afterword by Lorna Crozier • 2005 • xviii + 62 pp. • ISBN 978-0-88920-489-8
Christopher Dewdney	*Children of the Outer Dark: The Poetry of Christopher Dewdney*, edited by Karl E. Jirgens, with an afterword by Christopher Dewdney • 2007 • xviii + 60 pp. • ISBN 978-0-88920-515-4
Don Domanski	*Earthly Pages: The Poetry of Don Domanski*, edited by Brian Bartlett, with an afterword by Don Domanski • 2007 • xvi + 62 pp. • ISBN 978-1-55458-008-8

Louis Dudek *All These Roads: The Poetry of Louis Dudek*, edited by Karis Shearer, with an afterword by Frank Davey • 2008 • xx+ 70 pp. • ISBN 978-1-55458-039-2

Paul Dutton *Sonosyntactics: Selected and New Poetry by Paul Dutton*, edited by Gary Barwin, with an afterword by Paul Dutton • forthcoming 2015 • ISBN 978-1-77112-132-3

George Fetherling *Plans Deranged by Time: The Poetry of George Fetherling*, edited by A.F. Moritz, with an afterword by George Fetherling • 2012 • xviii + 64 pp. • ISBN 978-1-55458-631-8

Sky Dancer Louise Bernice Halfe *Sôhkêyihta: The Poetry of Sky Dancer Louise Bernice Halfe*, edited by David Gaertner, with an afterword by Sky Dancer Louise Bernice Halfe • 2018 • xx + 96 pp. • ISBN 978-1-77112-349-5

Phil Hall *Guthrie Clothing: The Poetry of Phil Hall, a Selected Collage* edited by rob mclennan, with an afterword by Phil Hall • 2015 • xvi + 72 pp. • ISBN 978-1-77112-191-0

Robert Kroetsch *Post-glacial: The Poetry of Robert Kroetsch,* selected with an introduction by David Eso and an afterword by Aritha van Herk • 2019 • xviii + 94 pp. • ISBN 978-1-77112-426-3

M. Travis Lane *The Crisp Day Closing on My Hand: The Poetry of M. Travis Lane*, edited by Jeanette Lynes, with an afterword by M. Travis Lane • 2007 • xvi + 86 pp. • ISBN 978-1-55458-025-5

Tim Lilburn *Desire Never Leaves: The Poetry of Tim Lilburn*, edited by Alison Calder, with an afterword by Tim Lilburn • 2007 • xiv + 50 pp. • ISBN 978-0-88920-514-7

Eli Mandel *From Room to Room: The Poetry of Eli Mandel*, edited by Peter Webb, with an afterword by Andrew Stubbs • 2011 • xviii + 66 pp. • ISBN 978-1-55458-255-6

Daphne Marlatt *Rivering: The Poetry of Daphne Marlatt*, edited by Susan Knutson, with an afterword by Daphne Marlatt • 2014 • xxiv + 72 pp. • ISBN 978-1-77112-038-8

Steve McCaffery *Verse and Worse: Selected and New Poems of Steve McCaffery 1989–2009*, edited by Darren Wershler, with an afterword by Steve McCaffery • 2010 • xiv + 76 pp. • ISBN 978-1-55458-188-7

Don McKay *Field Marks: The Poetry of Don McKay*, edited by Méira Cook, with an afterword by Don McKay • 2006 • xxvi + 60 pp. • ISBN 978-0-88920-494-2

Al Purdy *The More Easily Kept Illusions: The Poetry of Al Purdy*, edited by Robert Budde, with an afterword by Russell Brown • 2006 • xvi + 80 pp. • ISBN 978-0-88920-490-4

Sina Queyras	*Barking & Biting: The Poetry of Sina Queyras*, selected with an introduction by Erin Wunker, with an afterword by Sina Queyras • 2016 • xviii + 70 pp. • ISBN 978-1-77112-216-0
F.R. Scott	*Leaving the Shade of the Middle Ground: The Poetry of F.R. Scott*, edited by Laura Moss, with an afterword by George Elliott Clarke • 2011 • xxiv + 72 pp. • ISBN 978-1-55458-367-6
Fred Wah	*The False Laws of Narrative: The Poetry of Fred Wah*, edited by Louis Cabri, with an afterword by Fred Wah • 2009 • xxiv + 78 pp. • ISBN 978-1-555458-046-0
Tom Wayman	*The Order in Which We Do Things: The Poetry of Tom Wayman*, edited by Owen Percy, with an afterword by Tom Wayman • 2014 • xx + 92 pp. • ISBN 978-1-555458-995-1
Rachel Zolf	*Social Poesis: The Poetry of Rachel Zolf*, selected with an introduction by Heather Milne and an afterword by Rachel Zolf • 2019 • xviii + 80 pp. • ISBN 978-1-77112-411-9
Jan Zwicky	*Chamber Music: The Poetry of Jan Zwicky*, edited Darren Bifford and Warren Heiti, with a conversation with Jan Zwicky • 2014 • xx + 82 pp. • ISBN 978-1-77112-091-3